3-98

OU
SC

OUTSOURCING SOLUTIONS

Workplace
Strategies
That Improve
Profitability

CARLEEN NELSON-NESVIG

Rhodes & Easton
Traverse City, Michigan

Published by RHODES & EASTON
121 E. Front Street, 4th Floor, Traverse City, Michigan 49684

Publisher's Cataloging-in-Publication Data
Nelson-Nesvig, Carleen.
  Outsourcing solutions: workplace strategies that improve profitability/
Carleen Nelson-Nesvig. – Traverse City, MI: Rhodes & Easton, 1998.
      p.   ill.   cm.
  Includes bibliographical references and index.
  ISBN 1-890394-01-7
  1. Outsourcing employment. 2. Employment trends. 3. Subcontracting
  I. Title.
HD2365. N45   1998   97-00000
658.723 dc—21   CIP

PROJECT COORDINATION BY JENKINS GROUP, INC.

01 00 99 98   ◆   5   4   3   2   1

Printed in the United States of America

Dedicated

to

Michael, Matthew, Sarah, and Luke

Contents

Interns
Outsourcing Company
Part-time Work
Retirees
Seasonal Work
Temporary Employees
Temporary Work

To Rule or Not to Rule
Go with Your Strengths
Eliminate Human Resources?
Borrow or Lease Technology
Shop for Marketing Expertise
The Need for Flexibility
Meet Seasonal Needs
Responding to the Ups and Downs
Fixed vs. Variable Costs
Downsizing
Specialties
Make Time
Value-added Services
Time, Expertise, and Cost Savings

Why Workers Turn to Outsourcing
Why Workers Want to Be Their Own Boss

List of Figures

List of Tables

Preface

With unemployment at its lowest point in history, many American industries have turned to outsourcing some of their tasks and responsibilities; thus avoiding the need to hire additional employees.

Some say this has resulted in cost savings, expanded knowledge, increased efficiencies, and a myriad of other benefits that were not previously enjoyed by utilizing employees. Others believe that there is no cost savings when you factor in training, reduced production levels, and low morale. A third contingent would suggest that outsourcing is simply a fad — much like a quality improvement or management objective program.

The purpose of this book is to investigate outsourcing opportunities available in today's market and assist organizations in making well-educated decisions about whether or not outsourcing is the solution for them.

I have focused on identifying the kinds of organizational needs that are met, the positive and negative effects, and the critical factors in the evaluative process relative to outsourcing. Research concentrated on existing writings from periodicals, journals, and bulletins as well as studies completed by professional associations, universities, and consulting firms.

It is important that readers understand that the best possible worker option is when existing employees can be trained to fulfill the needs of their organization. In today's economy, businesses may, for a variety of reasons, be unable to employ employees with the necessary skills. When this is the case, outsourcing should be considered.

I believe that outsourcing has always played a role in our work force. While outsourcing has its limitations and liabilities, tremendous benefits can and do result for everyone when directed planning, research, and communication is provided to the outsourcer. Outsourcing will continue to play a role in the future of American industry and should be seriously considered as an alternative to traditional employer/employee relationships.

If you are interested in profiting from the utilization of the new American work force, reading this book is a must!

Acknowledgments

FIVE YEARS AGO, DR. C. K. KLINE, A PROFESSOR AT LANSING
Community College in Lansing, Michigan, introduced me to the
writings of John Naisbitt and Patricia Aburdene. These authors
prophesied a new direction in the American work force that included outsourcing options.

Authors like Joseph H. Boyett and Henry P. Conn (*Workplace
2000, The Revolution Reshaping American Business*), James A.
Belasco, Ph.D. (*Teaching the Elephant to Dance, The Manager's
Guide to Empowering Change,*) and Robert J. Kriegel and Louis
Patler (*If it Ain't Broke, Break it! And Other Unconventional
Wisdom for a Changing Business World*), all played a major role in
convincing me that to survive we must be better educated, prepared
for challenge, and ready to embrace change like never before.

Following their prophecies, I began an exploration of the possi-
bilities available for me to leave corporate America and create a new
place for myself as an entrepreneur. In 1993, I incorporated my own
human resource consulting firm and can happily say I have never
looked back.

If I hadn't believed then, what I believe today, "That outsourcing is our future," I would never have left what I perceived as a stable and comfortable position in human resource management to pursue a new and exciting life as an outsourcer.

As I watch fellow professionals struggling to find their niche, I am forever grateful that authors like these were available to me so that I could be a successful part of the new American work force.

On a state and local level, special thanks is given to the Michigan Chamber of Commerce, publisher of *A Michigan Employer's Guide to Flexible Staffing - Independent Contractors/Temporary Employees/Employee Leasing* by the Labor and Employment Relations Department of the Miller, Canfield, Paddock and Stone law firm for permission to excerpt and paraphrase portions of that publication. Readers are encouraged to consider this outstanding document as an additional resource. Patricia Claire, legal counsel for Bee Tree Consulting and attorney at law for Willingham and Cote, P.C., provided final review of legal issues contained in Chapter 8.

On a national level, my gratitude and respect to the Society of Human Resource Management (SHRM) for its permission to reprint and/or paraphrase from *HR Magazine,* as well as the SHRM Foundation for reprints from *The Contingent Worker, A Human Resources Perspective* by W. Gilmore McKie and Laurence Lipsett. The SHRM Foundation's role in the lives of human resource professionals places them on the cutting edge of their discipline and has elevated their positions to a new, respectable level.

On a personal level, I am especially appreciative of the tremendous support from my husband Ed Nesvig, who has from the beginning believed in me and my dreams. He was, is, and will always be the driver that keeps me going the distance. In pursuit of my goals, he and our daughter Sandra Silvasi (Casey), have sacrificed much in terms of my time away from them.

My deepest and most profound respect goes to friends and colleagues, Rhonda Kay Prokos, Fran Zatorski, and Marlo McCutcheon, whose word processing, editing, graphic tutelage, and encouragement helped me to verbalize my beliefs to our readers.

On a professional level I acknowledge my clients who are a part of the new American work force. Some not only participated in our survey on outsourcing but provided many of the articles referred to in this book, while others proofed our copy and added insight.

And finally I thank my editor (also an independent contractor), Mary Jane Eder of Chelsea, Michigan, who read and reread, added and deleted, and checked and rechecked — my eternal gratitude and respect for her devotion to her vocation and this book.

Thanks to all and God Bless You!

WARNING/DISCLAIMER

This book is designed to assist business professionals in designing, planning, and implementing flexible workplace and employee alternative solutions now and in the future.

It is not intended to pass judgment on traditional employer/employee relationships, offend occupations or classifications, or cast a negative light on labor movements where they are necessary due to tyrannical behaviors, unfair treatment, and/or employee abuse. It does not represent itself in any manner as offering legal or expert assistance to its readers. If legal or expert assistance is required, those services should be sought.

While every effort has been made to provide complete and accurate information, this topic is too extensive to rely on any one publication (even mine!). Readers are encouraged to refer to additional publications, footnotes, and resources made throughout this publication. We believe that reviewing these materials as well as ours will offer you a more thorough understanding of the issues involved.

The purpose of this book is to educate readers on the issues of outsourcing. The author and Bee Tree Consulting Ltd. shall have neither liability nor responsibility to any person or entity with respect to any loss or damage caused, or alleged, by the information provided in this book.

If you do not wish to be bound by the above, please return this book to the publisher for a full refund.

OUTSOURCING SOLUTIONS

1.

What is Outsourcing?

Outsourcing is about saving time, gaining expertise, and borrowing technology. It's about reacting quickly to changing markets in order to save money. It's about strategic planning and profitability. It's about breaking through organizational structures and focusing on business. It's about holding on and letting go at the same time. It's about the integration of old and new ideas and it's changing the way America does business.

Outsourcing is a wild and crazy ride — destination success.

Outsourcing is also about the new American work force. This work force is dynamic, powerful, eager, highly skilled, diverse, and driven. According to Peter F. Druker in his book, *Managing for the Future, the 1990's and Beyond*, "The productivity of the newly dominant groups in the work force...will be the biggest and toughest challenge facing managers in the developed countries for decades to come."[1] If this is the case, then identifying, understanding, re-cruiting, contracting, and obtaining the *most appropriate* workers as members of the work force is a first step in securing our country's future in global economic competitions.

If you add the dynamics of this new work force (i.e., increases in both female and minority participation, aging, better educated workers, illiteracy issues, shortages of labor, reorganization of work forces), then businesses are challenged to define when and where the roller coaster ride will stop.[2]

THE ADVANTAGES OF OUTSOURCING

Outsourcing has an advantage over traditional employee options because it is flexible. This flexibility is a buffer for businesses and allows them to keep up with or even surpass their competition.

Using the work force strategies in this book, you can lower your costs, improve your profit margin, save time, gain expertise, and simplify your processes.

To decide if outsourcing is the solution for you, you must have:

1. A clear definition of outsourcing;

2. An understanding of why outsourcing is used in today's business community;

3. A knowledge of the pros and cons of outsourcing; and

4. An understanding of why outsourcing is appropriate.

Only when these criteria are met will you be able to decide on the right strategies to improve your organization's profitability.

This book will help you:

1. Determine whether you should or should not outsource;

2. Decide what and when to outsource;

3. Manage your work force;

4. Understand legal and union issues;

5. Write a contract agreement that defines performance requirements and pricing criteria; and

6. Reap the greatest rewards from outsourcing.

Included in this book is the advice of corporate executives who have profited by outsourcing. In such areas as marketing, advertising, financial and/or human resources, these executives have used temporaries, independent contractors, interns, co-op's, and retirees to their benefit. By following the advice of these pioneers, other businesses can avoid costly mistakes.

Should your business invest in technologies, training, and human resources in areas that you don't need or want to maintain control? As your business conducts strategic planning, carefully consider outsourcing as an option when you review core competencies, values, and cultures.

2.

Defining Outsourcing and its Workers

THERE APPEARS TO BE CONFUSION ABOUT THE DEFINITION OF OUT-sourcing. Some professionals believe it is simply contingent workers or flexible staffing options. Others think it occurs whenever an organization outsources a specific function like security, payroll, or marketing. We would like to set the record straight by saying, "It's all of that and more…"

Outsourcing occurs anytime the organization elects to utilize outside, independent workers to conduct work-related tasks. The how, what, where, and when of the working conditions are driven by the needs of the organization and may vary from assignment-to-assignment, day-to-day, and worker-to-worker.

Independent workers are as varied (with varying degrees of skills, abilities, education, objectives, and titles) as the work they perform.

Here are just a few examples:

AGENCY TEMPORARIES

Hired through an agency, these workers are contracted on a case-by-case, hour-per-hour basis, throughout the year to function in the same or similar capacity as regular, full-time employees.

While temporary workers perform work for the outsourcing user and are exposed to their working conditions, schedules, and oftentimes work rules, they receive all remuneration (i.e., wages, benefits, withholdings, workers' compensation and unemployment compensation) from their employer (the agency).

It should also be noted that there is substantial reliance on agency temporaries for trial period employment or "temp to perm" assignments where small owners utilize temporary employees with the understanding that after 90 days, assuming satisfactory performance, that the temporary worker will be converted to employee status.

CONTINGENT WORKERS

Neither worker nor outsourcing user anticipate full-time regular employment. Work hours, scheduling, equipment training, supervision, and working conditions are not within the span of control of the contracting party.

CONTRACTING USER

The organization responsible for the selection and contracting of the worker(s).

CONTRACT WORKERS

These workers are contracted by the outsourcing user to provide products/services often outside of the user's core competencies.

Contracted workers have traditionally included attorneys, certified public accountants, search firms, physicians, security guards, janitors, and grounds maintenance workers.

CONTRACTED TECHNICAL WORKERS

Contracted technical workers are highly skilled workers such as engineers, designers, scientists, or management information systems analysts. These workers often engage in long-term contracts and may be involved in global travel.

CO-OP STUDENTS

These workers are students that alternate between work and school in an effort to obtain both theoretical and practical applications of knowledge and/or skills in their field of study.

DIRECTLY HIRED

Directly hired workers are obtained through prearranged agencies, colleges, organizations, and union halls. A direct-hire list could include past employees who have exhausted recall rights following work force reductions, retirees, disabled workers, apprentices, co-ops, etc.

EMPLOYEE LEASING

Employee leasing occurs any time an employer divests itself of its worker's liabilities (payroll, benefits, legal concerns) to a third party, or commissions a third party to provide employees on a regular full-time basis for a fee.[3]

In some cases the employer and the leasing company may be considered joint employers and share liability.

HOME-BASED WORKERS

These workers elect or are provided with the opportunity to work from their homes for one employer. Traditionally, these workers have been employed in telemarketing, word processing, computer, writing, stuffing envelopes, and/or other simple assembly.

INDEPENDENT CONTRACTORS

Independent contractors are workers that work independently of the contracting user. As independents, they must successfully pass the provisions of the Internal Revenue Service 20-Factor Test, providing their own equipment, office, training, benefits, supervision, marketing, advertising, and booked hours.

Independent contractors must conduct similar work for more than one employer.

INTERNS

An intern is a student who has completed sufficient schooling to be of use to an employer by participating in specific curriculum-related assignments involving surveys, administration, reporting, data analysis, etc.

OUTSOURCING COMPANY

This is an independent vendor company that specializes in a function of the business community such as marketing, public relations, financing, human resources, packaging, distribution, food service, security, landscaping, or janitorial services.

PART-TIME WORK

Part-time work is employment that is less than 35 hours per week, and represents more than 90% of the 365,000 jobs created in the United States in one month.[4]

RETIREES

These workers are mature and often well-qualified workers that have completed vesting periods or career assignments and opt to return to the work force for the added challenge or financial reasons.

SEASONAL WORK

When an organization has peaks and valleys in its work patterns, this can be categorized as seasonal work. Traditionally, seasonal work is the definition applied when the work is in connection with holiday commerce, summer vacations, and fall harvesting.

In agriculture, seasonal work includes summer/fall harvesting, canning, freezing, and the shipping that follows. The demand for retail cashiers, salespeople, and stock persons spikes during the holiday season. Seasonal work also includes summer jobs for students and temporary replacements for vacation coverage.[5]

5. Reprinted with permission of The Society of Human Resource Management Foundation from *The Contingent Worker. A Human Resources Perspective* by Gordon McKie and Laurence Lipsett, 1995.

TEMPORARY EMPLOYEES

Temporary employees are workers hired with the understanding that the hours and days of their employment are of a temporary nature, and may last days, weeks, or years depending upon the needs of the business. Temporary employees can be independent contractors, agency temporaries, retirees, summer co-ops, leased, and/or direct hire workers.

TEMPORARY WORK

Work of a temporary nature can include worker replacement issues such as medical, vacation, and holiday coverage; worker additions for increased production demand, special projects, or assignments; and work of a specialized nature that may not otherwise be available within the existing work force or does not demand the hours expected of a full-time worker.

> Please note that nowhere in our definitions does the word *employee* appear. If an employee/employer relationship exists between the two parties, this is not considered to be an act of outsourcing. Readers should be particularly sensitive to the usage of *worker* vs. *employee* and *outsourcing user (contractor)* vs. *employer*.

3.

Why Do Organizations Outsource?

O<small>UTSOURCERS</small> <small>OFFER</small> <small>ORGANIZATIONS</small> <small>MULTIPLE</small> <small>OPPORTUNITIES</small> and benefits not always inherent in hiring their own employees. Issues to consider may include:

To Rule or Not to Rule

According to some, decentralization (the ability to make major and minor decisions at all levels of the organization) is leading to massive outsourcing by large corporations. Decentralized operations are finding that outsourcing can streamline processes and actually help businesses survive the absence of corporate control.[6] Others feel it is best to start with a centralized operation before outsourcing and suggest common central administration functions, practices, and interpretation.[7] Either way, each offers its own set of positive and negative variables.

---

7. Reprinted with permission of *Workforce* (formerly *Personnel Journal*) from

For example, in larger corporations it might make sense to offer a centralized accounting, sales, engineering, or human resource function even though these functions do not represent core competencies for the organization. While one operation may not be financially able to support full-time administration, the totality of the organization could share the cost. The organization might, however, opt instead to outsource portions of the function on a smaller or more local level. Examples may include seasonal financial reports, independent sales representatives, payroll, or benefit administration.

GO WITH YOUR STRENGTHS

Research supports the fact that today's organizations do not want to own nonessential functions. Executives at National Staff Management, an employee leasing firm with offices in Michigan, Georgia, and Florida, have built the core competencies issue into their radio advertising with slogans like "Get Back to Business." The organization's president and CEO, Scott Slyfield, says that his clients want to concentrate on what they know and do best. Because National Staff Management can recruit and hire workers who can handle the complexities of employment law issues (which require recordkeeping, reporting, and tax-related work), this removes a significant burden for them. Scott adds that, "Today, if you are not outsourcing, your eye is not on the ball and someone else is going to get your business."[8]

ELIMINATE HUMAN RESOURCES?

Across all industries human resource functions are being eliminated,

---

"Successful Outsourcing Depends on Critical Factors" by Jennifer Laabs, Sept. 1993.

automated, or outsourced, as reported by Lynn Brenner in the March 1996 issue of *CFO*.[9]

According to Brenner, human resource departments have been reduced and/or re-engineered at 58% of large U.S. corporations. For example, she points to David Axson of The Hackett Group, an Ohio-based consulting firm, who reports that the leading cause of the reduction is "a significant gap between business strategy development and its translation to HR strategies." When 50% of a professional's time is spent on routine administrative tasks and only 10% on organizational changes necessary to meet the corporation's business strategy, it's time to outsource.[10]

Thomas A. Stewart, a reporter for *Fortune Magazine*, supports the outsourcing of human resources completely and candidly wrote, "Why not blow the sucker [Human Resource Department] up...Deep six it. Rub it out; eliminate, toss, obliterate, nuke it; give it the old heave ho, force it to walk the plank; turn it into road kill."[11]

John D. Cooper, disagrees with Stewart in his July 1996 issue of *Michigan Forward* and writes that in speaking with four professionals who work in the field, he feels that "the human resource function is essential for the small business...if it is to maintain a competitive advantage with people leading the way."[12]

Cooper feels that human resource professionals can and often are aligned with the organization's philosophy, and that human resource activities far and away exceed simple record keeping and administrative functions.[13]

And what about human resource communication systems so vital to serving the needs of the business? Can these be performed effectively by an outsider?

Some say yes, citing that attorneys have long been the authors of procedure manuals and handbooks and very often play a behind-the-scenes role on issues from company rules to disciplinary action.

Others argue that to do the right job in human resources you must be a part of the work force, have an unobstructed view of people, visions, strategies, and principles. Human resource professionals are often viewed by both management and the work force as the company conscience. What happens when the conscience is outsourced? Does the behavior change?

I believe the answer is yes. The conscience is more vivid, more audible, more recognizable, and more reactive.

Outsourcers enjoy a degree of unquestionable credibility, which allows organizations to willingly share what may be internally confidential. Organizations can avoid in-house politics, and save time and costs by confiding in an outsourcer. The outsourcer, at the same time, must act in a timely and professional manner to protect their contract from defaults, terminations, legal exposures, or loss of payment.

This is not an indictment of in-house human resource professionals. I truly believe that internal and external support is necessary to meet the demands of employee relations, special projects, and strategic planning.

BORROW OR LEASE TECHNOLOGY

In his 1995 edition of *Managing Information Technology in Turbulent Times*, author Louis Fried writes that "...twenty-five percent of Fortune 1000 companies outsource one or more information systems (IS) functions. However, only 22.7% indicate that they plan further outsourcing within the next year, and only 4% of these companies say they are committed to eventually outsourcing all IS functions."[14]

Fried speaks to lawsuits, countersuits, hanky-panky, extra and unforeseen charges, surrender of control, escalating costs, system failures, absence of business resumption plans, security and integrity issues, duplication issues and efforts, reluctance to adopt new technology, licensing fees, penalties, and poor performance reasons for their outsourcing decisions.[15]

Others feel that organizations really do want and need to buy technological knowledge, believing that utilization of computer science consultants will greatly improve their business capabilities and systems. Replacing homegrown, 1970's vintage systems is prompting many businesses and banks in particular, to outsource.[16]

Joyce Stackhouse of Stackhouse Office Solutions, a Chelsea, Michigan-based computer training and service firm, agrees and adds that most organizations need technology but not the full-time, overhead burden that goes along with it. They may have to "put out the bucks" for hardware, but it's more cost-effective to bring in outsiders to train or maintain workers, software, and systems.[17]

As Stackhouse observes, organizations are more receptive to outsiders with technological savvy. They lack prejudices, are absent internal agendas, and offer a fresher and more effective approach to the situation. Internal workers can get bogged down in having handled hardware and software a certain way. An outsourcer has seen it adapted, modified, and upgraded or is more aware of its full potential. Organizations can pull from all of the outsourcer's experience.[18]

According to President Dennis Berkey of the Lansing, Michigan-based Business Support Group (BSG), a major marketing advantage for his high tech computer hardware and software consulting firm is the ability for his organization to spread technology costs over the life of a client's contract. For BSG this includes the high costs of start-up.[19]

Others, like John Verity of *Business Week*, agree that organizations typically can "convert customers to newer, more useful systems while slashing technology costs by as much as 50%."[20]

SHOP FOR MARKETING EXPERTISE

Dennis Keith, president and CEO of Phoenix Concepts, a national marketing and consulting firm in Elk Grove Village, Illinois, built his entire company around outsourcing. Keith derives the majority of his clients from organizations that want marketing and advertising expertise from the experts. Keith says:

> For us, the number one goal is our client. We are going to do whatever it takes to make them happy. In today's economy, that often means one stop shopping. If my organization can provide a variety of services within that function, we will. That sometimes means we will collaborate, align, or outsource pieces of a project to other outsourcers with whom we have had a successful history.[21]

Keith feels that the key to successful outsourcing is commitment and adds that his firm insists on strong partnering ties that support the needs of all parties involved. This can mean longer hours, more communication, and in the end a lower cost, value-added product and service.[22]

THE NEED FOR FLEXIBILITY

Flexibility is a major reason organizations outsource and plays a key role in the continuing success of part-time workers. According to a 1992 study, part-time workers accounted for 41% of retail jobs, 29% of service industry jobs, and 27% of agricultural jobs. Finance and construction each employed 13%. Wholesale trade, manufacturing, transportation, and utilities represented smaller percentages.[23]

According to Olmsted and Smith in their book, *Creating a*

---

23. Reprinted with permission of The Society of Human Resource Management Foundation from *The Contingent Worker. A Human Resources Perspective* by Gordon McKie and Laurence Lipsett, 1995.

Flexible Workplace, "The entrance of women into the work force was accompanied by a demand for jobs that would allow them to meet the needs of their families."[24]

Karen Meyer-Bentley, human resource manager for Colorbok, located in Dexter, Michigan, insists that it was the need for flexibility that prompted her organization to secure what for them escalated to as many as 70 temporary workers during the summer of 1995 and 40 temporary workers in 1996.[25]

With unemployment dipping to some of the lowest percentages in decades, Meyer-Bentley (like many human resource professionals across the country), continues to face the daily challenge of finding good workers in a depleted market. Utilizing temporary workers allows organizations to retain workers during peak seasons and refer them back to the contracting agencies during slow times.

MEET SEASONAL NEEDS

Most companies say that contingent work forces help meet their often erratic staffing needs such as seasonality of work loads. According to Debra Iben, past director of Skill Tech Employment, a Lansing, Michigan-based temporary and leasing firm, using contingent or complementary workers helps minimize the impact of industry ups and downs on regular employees.[26]

An especially ripe area for outsourcing, say experts, is financial and human resource compliance. Because compliance is seasonal, in most cases, there isn't sufficient justification for having full-time staff people do compliance work. This means that auditing, year-end financials, and wrap ups should not be a fixed but a variable cost. Federal contractors could easily outsource the compilation of affirmative action plan data that requires once-a-year administration.[27]

27. Reprinted with the permission of *Workforce* (formerly *Personnel Journal*) from "Contingent Staffing Requires Serious Strategy" by Gillian Flynn, April 1995.

RESPONDING TO THE UPS AND DOWNS

Companies in growth or decline stages recognize the merits of being able to provide more for less. For years, organizations at all levels of maturity have contracted with outside firms to perform such functions as mail, payroll, security, data processing and other services.[28]

Today human resource professionals are benefiting from outsourcing functions such as recruitment, benefits communication, benefits plan design, retirement services, human resource record keeping services, employee assistance programs, 401K plans, medical-claims processing, transaction processing, relocation services, and awards and incentive programs.[29]

Bee Tree Consulting Ltd.'s survey indicates that while 35% of the respondents would utilize outsourcing during a start up business

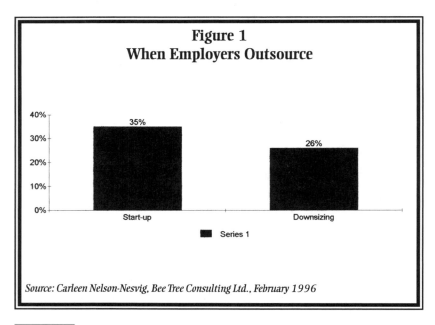

Figure 1
When Employers Outsource

Source: Carleen Nelson-Nesvig, Bee Tree Consulting Ltd., February 1996

---

28. Reprinted with the permisson of the publisher from "Addition by Subtraction
—Outsourcing Strengthens Business Focus" by James Spee from *HR Magazine*

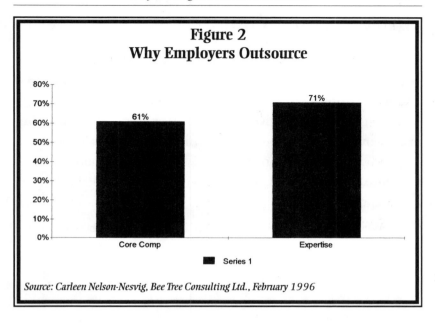

Figure 2
Why Employers Outsource

Source: *Carleen Nelson-Nesvig, Bee Tree Consulting Ltd., February 1996*

and 26% downsizing or rightsizing, the reasons in 71% of the cases would be to obtain expertise. Sixty-one percent reported the need to focus on core competencies [Figure 1 and Figure 2].

Many of the companies interviewed during our research indicated that outsourcing opportunities had been vital to their ability to compete in the marketplace during start-up business phases. Downsizing companies shared similar opinions but also attributed their utilization to costs.

Do organizations achieve the flexibility, cost efficiency, and value-added benefits they strive for? Some do and some don't. Let's consider them individually.

published by the Society of Human Resource Management, Alexandria, VA, March 1995.

29. Reprinted with the permission of *Workforce* (formerly *Personnel Journal*) from "Contingent Staffing Requires Serious Strategy" by Gillian Flynn, April 1995.

FIXED VS. VARIABLE COSTS

While some organizations say a company will outsource when they want to streamline the way their business operates — others say that it all comes down to cost. Martin J. Jerick, president of Lansing, Michigan-based Innovative Computer Services (an information man-agement and data processing firm that specializes in high tech approaches to database marketing data conversion and technical assistance), agrees and shared his organizations humble beginnings as evidence:

> Without outsourcing, we could not have grown to where we are today. I can still remember when we didn't have a letter shop or a laser printer and had two customers that needed that as a part of our service. We outsourced those components of the job, kept the customers happy and added the components when we had the funds and the necessity to do so.[30]

Today ICS continues to outsource all of its legal, financial, and human resource responsibilities in addition to selected areas of production, such as printing or simple assemblies like labeling. "We even contract for programmers from time-to-time," adds Jerick. "The economics make more sense! We have the image and resources of a large organization without the costs - awesome."[31]

Exhibits Now! President Suellen Parkes of a Warren, Michigan-based marketing exhibits firm, enthusiastically agrees with Jerick:

> It's a winning solution for me and my customer. We design and construct exhibits all over the country. It doesn't make sense to pay for material, space, machinery, and labor on a full-time basis for a part-time need. Many of our customers are one or two-person businesses. They are very cost conscious. We outsource our work to contractors with low overhead, their costs are reasonable, and we can pass on better pricing to our customers![32]

Parkes' company moved to leased employees after trying the traditional employee option, and today enjoys its impact on her company's bottom line. Parkes talks about increased benefit options for her workers, lower MESC rates, free seminars, COBRA, ADA, and FICA administration, time savings, and other savings.[33]

Organizations have learned fixed costs versus variable work load lessons. In an ever increasing demand to change costs into revenues by incorporating a value-added mentality, organizations are more and more willing to mix inside and outside resources for bottom-line results.

How are these cost savings derived? The probabilities are endless and begin with labor costs, continuity, training, knowledge, time savings, higher quality, and no loss of investment for technological changes, etc. Some studies suggest the average savings to be around 10% with unlimited sets of variables.[34]

National Staff Management president and CEO Slyfield says:

> Savings are hard to pinpoint. For example, in our field it depends on how effectively you use our safety programs, techniques, and structure. Obviously, if you do, you will save money. The industry average for direct/indirect employer costs can range from 5% to 20%. This includes some subjective administrative costs. Because we underwrite our companies, we are always looking for red flags that indicate long-term risks. Eliminating those risks could also mean substantial savings.[35]

Slyfield feels one of the most positive effects of leasing is the budgeting discipline it provides. "Start-up organizations fail because they start out on a shoe string, anticipate for operating expenses, but totally overlook the overhead inherent in hiring employees." Slyfield explains that, "having a good budgeting strategy with outsourcing partners that know the game and how to play it has helped many of our clients stay in business."[36]

DOWNSIZING

Many believe that downsizing efforts over the last decade have been too extensive at cutting into core competency areas and have thus forced organizations to either hire back previous workers as either independent contractors or temporary employees (or search for new employees to replace them at higher costs).[37] Others are turning to staffing companies to avoid these costs and IRS headaches, as well as bad feelings.

As organizations continue to downsize, re-engineer, and break through the barriers, professionals will continue to find ways of adding value (but not cost) by outsourcing. Many of those professionals utilize traditional recruiting beliefs, worker recycling processes, as well as good business sense and will look to workers who might be affected by work force reductions, retirements or disabilities in an effort to save both workers and dollars.

After all, why pay unemployment severance, disability payments, and replacement costs when repackaging, shuffling, re-scheduling, redefining, and redesigning the work force can benefit everyone?[38]

SPECIALTIES

Today small niche businesses appear to be competing and winning in the outsourcing bidding wars.

In 1992, Dallas County awarded Systems and Computer Technology (a $91 million outsourcing and software company) a seven-year, $35 million outsourcing contract because they were more specialized than the county's long-standing outsourcer, Electronic Data Systems.[39]

---

38. Reprinted with permission of the publisher from "Staff to Suit" by Phaedra Brotherton from *HR Magazine*, published by the Society of Human Resource Management, Alexandria, VA, December 1995.

Owens & Minor, a wholesaler of hospital supplies specializing in the warehousing, inventory, and supply components of hospital supplies, saved South Miami Homestead Hospital $200,000 one year after signing on, because they could maintain inventories and offer discounts unavailable to the general public.[40]

Security firms have enjoyed a healthy market share for specializing in guard and investigative services.

MAKE TIME

Today's organizations do not want to own nonessential functions. "According to a study recently released by Lincolnshire, Illinois-based Hewitt Associates titled *Employers Experience in Outsourcing*, time is the main reason that employers want to outsource. More than a third (37%) of those surveyed said that the time they'd save was their foremost consideration in making the decision to outsource..."[41]

The Williamston, Michigan-based leader of blow-molding machines, Bekum America Corporation's President Martin Stark agrees:

> Outsourcing a portion of our human resource functions has provided us with products and services that time had never allowed for. Our human resource "things to do list" got longer every year and management and employees got more frustrated. In 1996, we elected to outsource our list and in less than nine months, have completed major projects, like employee opinion surveys, position descriptions, compensation structures, performance and communication programs. With these activities, we can see morale and productivity

41. Reprinted with the permission of *Workforce* (formerly *Personnel Journal*) from "Successful Outsourcing Depends on Critical Factors" by Jennifer Laabs, September 1993.

improvements. Employees can see what we are doing on their behalf. It's been a win-win for everyone.[42]

VALUE-ADDED SERVICES

Perhaps of equal importance to companies was the issue of value-added services as shown in a survey by Bee Tree Consulting Ltd. in February, 1996 [Figure 3].

According to Dianne Mitchell, human resource manager for the Lansing-based company, National Legal Labs and Group Benefit Services, she wanted noncore business in expert hands and is especially appreciative of the outsourcers available to her organization. Mitchell adds that outsourcers also save her from keeping up on nonessential competencies, equipment, material costs, and compliance issues.[43]

Human resource professional Scott Derthick, of Lansing, Michigan-based Peckham Vocational Industries, says internal workers are often perceived as management employees that are on the

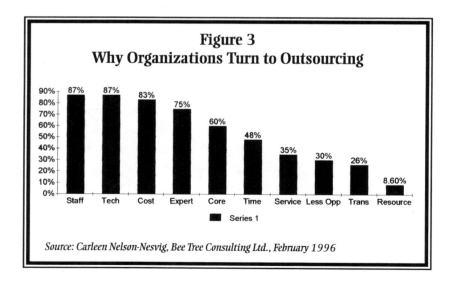

Figure 3
Why Organizations Turn to Outsourcing

Source: Carleen Nelson-Nesvig, Bee Tree Consulting Ltd., February 1996

company payroll — willing to do what they perceive management wants them to do as opposed to what should be done.[44]

Organizations say objectivity (the ability to take a fresh, unbiased look at a problem), is one of the greatest values of outsourcing.

Phoenix Concepts President Dennis Keith offers what they refer to as "out of the box" thinking in its marketing illustration. According to Keith, companies turn to his organization for marketing, product, and service ideas to avoid "in the box" or internal group think results. Keith adds that internal workers are often lost in a maze or can't see the big picture. Outsourcers have an unobstructed view of what is going on or what is needed.[45]

TIME, EXPERTISE, AND COST SAVINGS

What are the major reasons organizations turn to outsourcing? According to a 1993 Hewitt Associates study cited in *Personnel Journal*, the most commonly cited reason for outsourcing human

**Illustration 1
Out of the box—Phoenix Concepts**

resources is to save time (37%), gain expertise (18%), reduce cost (14%), supplement staffing (14%), reduce hassle (13%), minimize complexity (12%), provide added service (11%), enhance administration (6%), and focus on core business (6%).[46]

According to the Bee Tree Consulting Ltd. survey, there is no question that cost (83%), expertise (75%), and time (48%) advantages were among the main reasons to outsource [Figure 3, see page 46].

Our survey also suggests the following reasons: supplement staffing needs (87%), acquire technology (87%), concentrate on core business (60%), increase service (35%), reduce opportunity for failure (30%), transparent to customers/employees (26%), and gain an added resource (8.6%).

Another source, "National Survey on Outsourcing Human Resource Services" by Linkage Inc., shows that most organizations outsource to use the expertise of specialists (88%), to save time (54%), reduce costs (41%), save administrative costs (38%), focus on core business (30%), function not part of the core business (26%), increased responsibilities (21%), and reduced liability (7%) [Figure 4, see page 49].[47]

While the previous three surveys do not agree on everything, all three support that time, expertise, and cost are the top three reasons why outsourcing has become a part of doing business in the U.S. In fact, of those surveyed, over 80% outsource parts of their business activities, and nearly 75% said they have no plans to change that approach.

A few words of caution are needed, however. In another survey conducted by The Society of Human Resource Management (SHRM) summarizing contingent labor costs in three separate companies, only one actually saved money as a result of keeping training costs relatively low. The survey also suggests a 7% drop in productivity with outsourcing, which should be factored into the cost effectiveness equation.

The February 1993 supplement to *Business and Legal Reports Inc.*, in its section on "Why Use Temporary Employees?" says:

> It used to be that temporary employment was confined to workers hired to fill in for vacationing employees or those on sick leave. Today, alternatives to regular full-time personnel abound, and can make it possible for employers to remain lean and flexible. The use of temporary workers allows them scheduling responsiveness, saves benefit costs, often reduces training, alleviates overloads, accommodates one-time projects, and prevents a succession of expensive and traumatic hires and layoffs. While most companies hire only a few temporary workers at a time, some firms may lease entire work forces on a quasi-permanent basis.[48]

John P. Kotter (1995) in his book, *The New Rules - How to Succeed in Today's Post-Corporate World*, writes:

> Where we are today [in 1992] is a vast improvement over two decades ago. The corporation is very different now. It is

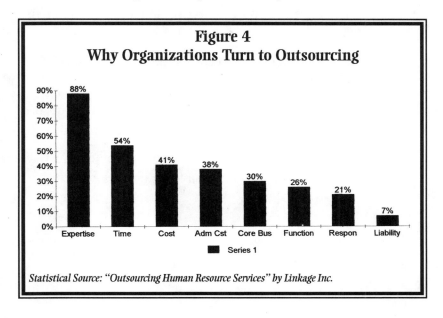

Figure 4
Why Organizations Turn to Outsourcing

Statistical Source: "Outsourcing Human Resource Services" by Linkage Inc.

leaner, flatter and less bureaucratic. Because some linkages inside the company have been loosened while others outside the corporation have been strengthened, the firm is more externally focused. Quality, productivity, and profits are up.[49]

He suggests that even though employment inside the firm is down significantly, the employment outside the corporation has increased, now restructured from a huge and rigid organizational pyramid, to a coalition of smaller and flatter units, both inside and outside the official boundaries.[50]

His writings, and those of other researchers, predict that hierarchical pyramids will either disappear completely or become shorter, smaller, and less rigid in an effort to become more versatile, cost competitive, and innovative in this era of global competition.

Such a change in corporate America's organizational structure will make it difficult to operate without the use of outsourcing.

Kotter offers the following reasons that organizations outsource today:

1. Outsourcers are more objective and less caught in the myopia of strong corporate cultures.

2. They are not locked into corporation "group think" conditions.

3. They are less threatened as messengers to offer up bad news.

4. They can specialize in certain kinds of problems in ways that are economically impossible for insiders.[51]

---

49. Reprinted with the permission of The Free Press, a division of Simon & Schuster from *The New Rules: How to Succeed in Today's Post-Corporate World* by John P. Kotter, 1995.

50. Ibid

51. Ibid

4.

Positive Effects of Outsourcing

THERE IS NO QUESTION THAT OUTSOURCING WORK ALLOWS ORGANIzations to concentrate on core competencies while transferring employee costs and liabilities to a third party. Because of advances in technology, outsourcing users can package entire administrative services, sell them to the lowest, most qualified bidder and still keep the outsourcing options transparent to the customer.[52]

Transferring costs are not the only benefits.

In Hewitt Associate's survey [see page 47], 18% of those responding felt that outsourcing had expanded the intellectual pool and 12% said outsourcing eliminated complex functions internally.[53]

Executive Director Hank Van Kampen of Kandu Industries, a Holland, Michigan-based rehabilitation agency, feels value is added and says that he enjoys the ability to subsidize his resource pool with human resource professionals, certified public accountants, and

---

52. Reprinted with the permission of the publisher from "Addition by Subtraction—Outsourcing Strengthens Business Focus" by James Spee from

attorneys that may be better equipped to make decisions involving compliance issues.[54]

Organizations and government regulations are fundamentally changing. Keeping up with core competencies is challenging enough without the added burden of issues outside of the core business. Transferring the work inherently eliminates most training requirements, thereby subjugating training and development costs.

Organizations may also use outsourcers to conduct training of in-house personnel, top management executives, and/or front-line supervision. Outsourcing provides the opportunity to complete projects under budget and ahead of schedule. Organizations can take advantage of their outsourcers' expertise by hiring the outsourcers on an internal or external basis. By working closely with their outsourcers, they can have cutting edge programs and their staff will understand how the programs were created or maintained.

Because outsourcing firms are typically specialists in their field, they tend to provide a much better product and/or service than what traditionally has been available in-house. Consistency of application, procedure, and low error ratios are reflective of the specialist's drive for detail.

Assignments are often completed in less time than those delegated internally because outsourcing eliminates dealing with the everyday business-related or core competency issues. Processes are typically streamlined by outsourcing firms in an effort to cut costs, reduce errors and improve efficiencies. Organizations that use out-

---

HR Magazine, published by the Society of Human Resource Management, Alexandria, VA, March 1995.

53. Reprinted with the permission of *Workforce* (formerly *Personnel Journal*) from "Successful Outsourcing Depends on Critical Factors" by Jennifer Laabs, September 1993.

54. Ibid

sourcing have experienced high levels of staffing flexibility with the ability to obtain workers on an as-needed basis.

Innovation is a value-added enhancement to many outsourced projects when experts become more and more comfortable with the services they provide and reach for higher levels of service. Delivery dates are usually met or brought in ahead of schedule because the outsourcing agency doesn't get paid in full until the project is completed.

Confidentiality can also play a role in decisions to outsource. Employee assistance programs, career counseling and assessments, employee opinion surveys, and similar programs are all better received by participants if conducted by a third party practitioner.

5.

Negative Effects of Outsourcing

OUR RESEARCH ALSO INDICATES THAT OUTSOURCING, IF NOT CARE-fully strategized, can have a multitude of negative effects. New York City-based Towers Perrin found in a survey on outsourcing within the benefit function, that problems include:

1. lack of knowledge;

2. costs too difficult to judge;

3. high level of bureaucracy;

4. difficulties in obtaining consensus on design policies issued;

5. extensive staffing constraints;

6. no direct reporting relationship;

7. too task oriented;

8. unsatisfactory handling of complaints;

9.   turnover; and

10. poor quality and communication.[55]

Various other surveys cite the following concerns:

1.   loss of control over services;

2.   lack of relationships;

3.   need to supervise efforts;

4.   vendor complacency;

5.   inflation over time;

6.   lack of company identity; and

7.   perceived threat to workers.

Fifty percent of corporate staffs view outsourcing as a threat, said Jennifer Laabs in her *Personnel Journal* article, "Successful Outsourcing Depends on Critical Factors". These staffs expressed concern that their companies would lose control of their particular function or project.[56]

Organizations also expressed concern about hard-to-measure assignments and high start-up costs. There is a stress factor in keeping contingent workers on long enough to get a return on the investment while ensuring they don't become permanent employees.[57]

According to 70% of the employers surveyed during a study conducted by Bee Tree Consulting, a lack of knowledge about the company and how it operates was their biggest concern. Many felt it resulted in lost time and higher error ratio, 35% felt vendors grew

---

56. Reprinted with the permission of *Workforce* (formerly *Personnel Journal*) from "Successful Outsourcing Depends on Critical Factors" by Jennifer Laabs, September 1993.

57. Reprinted with the permission of *Workforce* (formerly *Personnel Journal*) from "Contingent Staffing Requires Serious Strategy" by Gillian Flynn, April 1995.

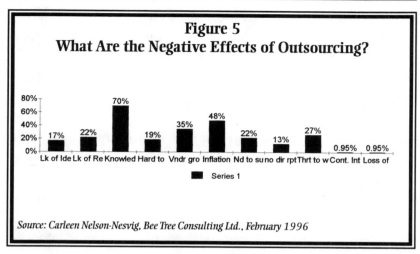

Figure 5
What Are the Negative Effects of Outsourcing?

Source: *Carleen Nelson-Nesvig, Bee Tree Consulting Ltd., February 1996*

complacent over time, and 17% said the outsourcers did not identify with their organization. Twenty-two percent expressed a lack of relationship with their organization, 27% perceived a threat to current workers, and 22% cited a need to supervise on a regular basis as negatives [Figure 5].

Other negative effects include concerns for security as it relates to proprietary information and an organization's ability to protect their competitive advantage.

Also, of concern to those who utilize contingent workers is work force harmony. Workers tend to fall into two tiers: the full-timers who enjoy the rights and privileges of employees (full benefits, employment security, training, and advancement) and contingent workers who, in many outsourcing firms, enjoy none of those benefits. Over time, if two people perform similar work with substantially different terms and conditions, the workers with less can become discontented or indifferent. The solution is to pay the same rates.

Contingent workers can also be less flexible than permanent workers. Independent contractors and part-time employees often set their own work schedules and may or may not receive the same training as permanent employees. Since turnover is high among contingent workers, companies may be reluctant to invest in training programs for them. This can limit cross-functional contributions or create inefficiencies in work processes.

Some organizations suggest that savings from outsourcing can be hard to measure or fleeting and offer horror stories to support this theory. Pre-packaged programs, obsolete software, out-of-date systems, processes or approaches, and one-fits-all mentalities (that afford the outsourcer standardized benefits), can cost the organization time, money and know-how.

Outsourcers quickly defend themselves by saying the information and/or directions they receive while on assignments are frequently vague or poorly communicated — that goals, objectives, and organization strategies are often poorly defined. These negatives can be avoided if organizations stick to a few simple rules:

1. If the outsourcer doesn't conduct a needs analysis - walk away;

2. Look for pre-packaged indicators, such as quick-fixes;

3. Check references and get specific details about what this outsourcer actually did for the company; and

4. Insist on trial periods before you agree to a full contract.

A side issue, but very much a common occurrence, is inflationary pricing as is evidenced by organizations like those in the health care industry. Contracts can begin at one cost, and a few years later, increase in price considerably. Retainer programs widely used by certified public accounts, attorneys, and search firms have also left a bad taste when organizations are unable to define what their retainer really paid for.

In addition to the issues already cited, the following problems are also identified:

1.   Possible litigation

2.   Transition costs (start-up/close out)

3.   Ethics issues, including conflict of interest

4.   Added or unforeseen charges

5.   Equipment and/or process upgrades

6.   Business interruption/resumption costs

7.   Need for and often lack of duplication

8.   Third-party delays

9.   Penalties

10. Lack of performance

11. Sole source procurement dangers

6.

Contingent Workers and Their Characteristics

Technically speaking, contingent workers can be:

1. agency temporaries;

2. contracted workers;

3. directly hired;

4. leased employees;

5. temporary employees; or

6. outplaced workers looking for full-time positions.

They are workers who desire flexibility and career development that full-time permanent positions do not offer.

They are workers who recognize that industry is fundamentally changing and that they cannot rely on large corporations for lifetime careers.

They are students, homemakers, retirees, and underemployed workers who want and need to subsidize their incomes.

They are workers who "like coming in and saving the world and then heading off and doing it again somewhere else," according to Gillian Flynn in his *Personnel Journal* article, "Contingent Staffing Requires Serious Strategy."[58]

Gone are the days when temporaries were just blue-collar or clerical staff. Today temporaries include interim executives such as doctors, lawyers, scientists and engineers. They are workers with long track records of leadership, who know how and when to make decisions.[59] They are workers willing to pay for their own benefits, work long hours, and often receive less pay in exchange for more freedom.

Retirees are also joining the contingent work force in the hundreds. According to Nicholas L. Reding, vice chairman of the Monsanto Company, headquartered in St. Louis, Missouri, his organization saved substantial costs in 1993 by creating the Retiree Resource Corporation (RRC).

Since 1991, RRC has been the preferred source for temporary workers "where retirees come in and hit the ground running." In addition to the savings and efficiency, RRC says that retirees already understand organizational climates; the way things are done. Retirees are mature, dependable, and have the ability to see what needs to be accomplished.[60]

What are the characteristics of contingent workers and others who offer outsourcing services such as independent contractors, part-time, seasonal, temporary, home-based, students, co-ops, interns, leased, and retirees?

According to a U.S. Bureau of Labor Statistics contingent work force study (February 1995), 26.3% of contingent workers were 25 to 34 years old, 49.6% male, 50.4% female, 80.9% white, 13.3% black, and 11.3% Hispanic [Table 1, see page 63]; 14.0% had less than a high school diploma, 27.9% were high school graduates, 31.2% had less than a bachelor's degree and 27.0% were college graduates [Table 2, see page 64].

---

58. Reprinted with the permission of *Workforce* (formerly *Personnel Journal*) from "Contingent Staffing Requires Serious Strategy" by Gillian Flynn, April 1995.

Table 1
Age and Race Distribution of Contingent Work Force

Characteristic	Contingent workers			Noncontingent workers
	Estimate 1*	Estimate 2	Estimate 3	
Age and Sex				
Total 16 years and over	100.0	100.0	100.0	100.0
16 to 19 years	16.6	15.2	10.7	4.3
20 to 24 years	25.0	22.2	19.8	9.6
25 to 34 years	26.0	27.5	26.3	26.1
35 to 44 years	18.5	19.8	21.0	28.0
45 to 54 years	8.2	9.5	12.6	19.8
55 to 64 years	3.8	3.7	5.9	9.4
65 years and over	1.8	2.1	3.7	2.8
Men, 16 years and over	49.3	49.3	49.6	54.0
16 to 19 years	7.2	6.8	4.8	2.2
20 to 24 years	12.0	10.7	9.7	5.2
25 to 34 years	12.9	13.6	13.8	14.3
35 to 44 years	10.0	10.3	10.2	15.1
45 to 54 years	3.3	4.2	5.7	10.5
55 to 64 years	2.6	2.4	3.6	5.1
65 years and over	1.2	1.3	1.9	1.7
Women, 16 years and over	50.7	50.6	50.4	46.0
16 to 19 years	9.5	8.4	5.9	2.1
20 to 24 years	13.0	11.5	10.1	4.4
25 to 34 years	13.1	13.9	12.5	11.8
35 to 44 years	8.5	9.5	10.8	12.9
45 to 54 years	4.9	5.3	6.9	9.3
55 to 64 years	1.2	1.3	2.3	4.3
65 years and over	0.6	0.8	1.8	1.2
Race and Hispanic origin				
White	80.0	80.1	80.9	85.6
Black	13.9	13.6	13.3	10.5
Hispanic Origin	13.6	12.9	11.3	8.3

NOTE: Noncontingent workers are those who do not fall into any estimate of "contingent" workers. Details for the above race and Hispanic-origin groups will not sum to totals because data for the "other races" group are not presented and Hispanics are included in both the white and black population groups.
Details for other characteristics may not sum to totals due to rounding.
*BLS used three alternative sets of assumptions about which factors constitute contingent employment.

Source: *Bureau of Labor Statistics, Bureau of National Affairs Inc., February 1995*

Table 2
Educational Attainment of Contingent Work Force

Characteristics	Contingent workers			Noncontingent
	Estimate 1*	Estimate 2	Estimate 3	workers
School enrollment				
Total, 16 to 24 years (thousands)	1142.0	1279.0	1841.0	16215.0
Percent	100.0	100.0	100.0	100.0
Enrolled	55.3	53.7	58.1	38.4
Not enrolled	44.7	46.3	41.9	61.6
Less than a high school diploma	12.2	13.4	11.4	9.4
High school grad, no college	13.7	14.5	15.7	27.8
Less than a bachelor's degree	10.3	10.0	8.5	17.0
College graduates	8.5	8.3	6.4	7.4
Educational attainment				
Total, 25 to 64 years (thousands)	1547.0	2070.0	3968.0	97633.0
Percent	100.0	100.0	100.0	100.0
Less than a high school diploma	14.0	13.6	12.0	9.6
High school grad, no college	27.9	27.5	27.3	32.4
Less than a bachelor's degree	31.2	31.3	27.5	29.0
College graduates	27.0	27.7	33.2	28.9

NOTE: Noncontingent workers are those who do not fall into any estimate of "contingent" workers. Detail may not sum to totals due to rounding.
*BLS used three alternative sets of assumptions about which factors constitute contingent workers.

Source: Bureau of Labor Statistics, Bureau of National Affairs Inc., February 1995

Temporary employee classifications offer comparable figures with 29% of the contingent work force between the ages of 25 and 34, as noted in a 1994 *Personnel Journal* survey [Figure 6, see page 65].

Comparable figures are also noted for protected class distribution with the highest percentage for white (80%), followed by black (11%); Hispanic (6%); Asian (2%); and physically challenged (1%) [Figure 7, see page 65].

Educational breakdowns within the temporary classifications cite that 73% have more than a high school education, 11% have attended a business or trade school, 28% have attended some college, and 17% have received a bachelor's degree [Figure 8, see page 66].

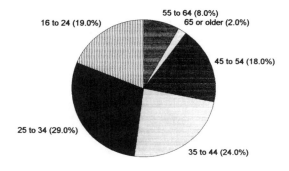

Figure 6
Temporary Services Age Distribution Characteristics

55 to 64 (8.0%)
65 or older (2.0%)

16 to 24 (19.0%)

45 to 54 (18.0%)

25 to 34 (29.0%)

35 to 44 (24.0%)

Statistical Source: Brenda Paik Sunoo, Personnel Journal, *July 1994*

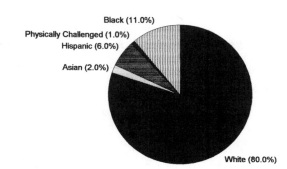

Figure 7
Temporary Services
Protected Class Distribution Characteristics

Black (11.0%)

Physically Challenged (1.0%)
Hispanic (6.0%)

Asian (2.0%)

White (80.0%)

Statistical Source: Brenda Paik Sunoo, Personnel Journal, *July 1994*

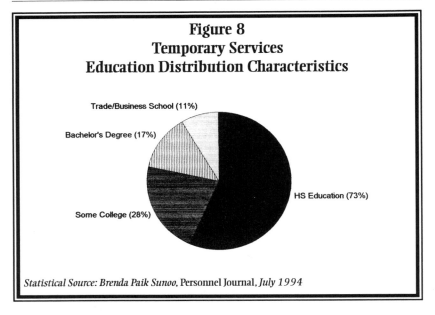

Figure 8
Temporary Services
Education Distribution Characteristics

Statistical Source: Brenda Paik Sunoo, Personnel Journal, *July 1994*

WHY WORKERS TURN TO OUTSOURCING

"Technology has transformed the way Americans work, the opportunities are unprecedented — to start a business, telecommute, invent new roles at the office, etc.," said Amy Saltzman, in her article, "You, Inc." which appeared in the October 1996 issue of *U.S. News & World Report.*[61]

"America has leapt headlong into the Information Age and our careers will never be the same...As technology allows companies to accomplish more with fewer people — millions of people will find themselves working for 'one-person' companies," according to Saltzman.[62]

Technology has given these companies the power to accomplish many (if not all) of the high-powered tasks that were once only handled by big corporations with many employees. It is predicted that "one-person" companies may be the fastest growing employment segment in the economy.

WHY WORKERS WANT TO BE THEIR OWN BOSS

The needs of dual-career families for flexibility and family value concerns have promoted new found interest in workers staying close to home, said Kerry Hannon, a contributor for *U.S. News & World Report*. Add the "trimming of corporate America," tax advantages of entrepreneurial endeavors, and recent government involvement in the need for portable benefit packages and workers are hard pressed to rely on a single employer for their income.[63]

According to the Small Business Administration, which counts new filings for employee identification numbers, people starting new businesses increased from 609,812 in 1984 to 819,477 in 1995.

Not surprisingly, many graduate students are inclined to select consulting positions because they offer a salary at 15% to 20% higher than other job offers. This is quite an incentive for those still paying college loans or beginning a family. Other graduates select consulting because of the very nature of the jobs themselves. They are less bureaucratic and offer smaller hierarchies. Some consultants are self-employed entrepreneurs and have no boss. The jobs are challenging, offering both growth and intellectual significance. Many are being asked to help organizations "survive and prosper by becoming more competitive," according to John Kotter in his book, *The New Rules - How to Succeed in Today's Post-Corporate World*.[64]

While all of this may sound glamorous to those "9 to 5" workers that brave the establishment day in and day out, many outsourcers are also quick to point out some of the less attractive characteristics of outsourcing:

---

64. Reprinted with the permission of The Free Press, a division of Simon Schuster from *The New Rules: How to Succeed in Today's Post-Corporate World*, by John P. Kotter, 1995.

1. Juggling Act - Outsourcers are often required to wear multiple hats or perform multiple projects at the same time.

2. Work Imbalance/Lack of Security - Work as an outsourcer can be feast or famine. One day it can't all get done. The next day, there's nothing to do.

3. Daily Testing - Outsourcers are required to prove themselves every day in every way.

4. Irregular/Poorly Defined Schedules - Depending on the assignment, contingent workers may work a variety of shifts, schedules, and times with little or no notice.

5. Fast Paced - Outsourcing is a fast paced career that requires the ability to adapt, think and react quickly. For this reason it tends to be more stressful.

6. Payment - Payments can be withheld until a project is completed, payments are sometimes delinquent, or difficult to collect.

7.

Managing the Outsourcer

MAXINE RICHMOND, AREA MANAGER FOR FLORIDA-BASED OFFICES of ADECCO (previously ADIA and ECCO) and now the biggest name in the staffing world, says that organizations contact ADEC-CO for "any and all" staffing needs.[65] There is no definitive organization that outsources; no single reason to outsource.

This full-service firm offers temporary, temp-to-hire, direct hire, and payroll services for its clients. Typically, these workers handle projects, vacation relief, maternity, and seasonal situations. While Richmond feels that temporary employees are becoming more and more popular to organizations of all sizes, she is quick to add that this trend is not an evasive process to forestall adding employees but a transitional process to predict future behavior by watching worker performance before making a hiring decision.[66]

Her words of advice to those considering decisions to outsource include:

1. Identify your reasons for outsourcing first.

2. Determine goals, skills, experience required.

3. Consider other requirements such as federal contracting, ISO 9002.

4. Look at short/long-term costs and effects (positive and negative).

5. Remember that agency temporaries are employed by the agency and not your organization. Let the agency handle the issues.

6. Give all of the workers good direction (Richmond says the single biggest influence in outsourcing failure is lack of communication).

7. Check the product/service regularly.

8. Say what you mean and mean what you say. Follow through on promises and threats.

9. Network with others who use outsourcing strategies. Learn from their mistakes.

10. Insist that your outsourcer adjust to your needs, just as your organization adjusts to the needs of its customers.[67]

Other organizations agree and add: (1) Watch for contractors that want to "unbundle" everything by adding charges over time for labor, equipment, training, or overtime, and (2) watch for agreements that include the right to re-open or charge for already agreed upon adjustments such as inflation. (3) Address renewal and termination conditions and insist on language that will guarantee smooth, professional, and pleasant transitions for everyone concerned. (4) Require and play an active role in all disaster recovery, security, and auditing programs. (5) Insist on ownership and liability statements, obtain copies of certifications, licenses, and insurance and always, always verify references.

A national survey of top level human resource professionals on outsourcing human resource services done by Linkage Inc., suggests taking a "strategic approach to outsourcing" by breaking down each service into its three aspects — strategic, operations, and maintenance — and then asking which aspects of the service should be outsourced.[68]

James Spee offers similar advice in his 1995 *HR Magazine* article, "Addition by Subtracting, Outsourcing Strengthens Business Focus":

1. "To make the quality and price comparisons between vendors easier, set benchmarks based on your current internal costs and quality levels." Then compare.

2. Agree on the meaning of performance standards. "Agreement on meaning is important, because lack of clarity may allow either the company or the service provider to reinterpret terms and conditions to its advantage."

3. If the task the organization is considering for outsourcing "requires specialized time or money investments, such as on-the-job training, special equipment, or long-term relationships", outsourcing may be very risky.

4. Put in safeguards to prevent the vendor from unfairly increasing prices.

5. Look for ways to make services tangible by requiring reports, letters of correspondence, milestone charts, etc.

6. Maintain a high level trust relationship with your provider.[69]

Other outsourcing practitioners suggest that organizations in-

---

69. Reprinted with the permission of the publisher from "Addition by Subtraction—Outsourcing Strengthens Business Focus" by James Spee from *HR Magazine*, published by the Society of Human Resource Management, Alexandria, VA, March 1995.

clude contract language that allows the organization to opt out of the arrangement for non-compliance. However, they caution that it can take time to work out the bugs of a new process and, even more importantly, consideration should be given for the learning curve while the new vendor tries to better understand the internal workings (procedures, goals, philosophy) of the organization.

Many organizations encourage vendors to work under a performance-based compensation arrangement, requiring reports, face-to-face contact, updates, site measurements, and time lines. Unbundling costs, providing line item descriptions, expenses and costs, as well as providing partial payments or pay down programs, can be great incentives for outsourcers to only charge for real costs and provide real performance.

Something everyone agrees on is the need to control those providing the outsourcing. In the end it is the organization that is responsible for the outsourced product and/or service. Staying on top, overseeing both process and results is critical to the success of any outsourcing project.

According to Stanley Nollen and Helen Axel, authors of *Managing Contingent Workers - How to Reap the Benefits and Reduce the Risks*, you must:
Control the size of the contingent staff:

1.   Prevent excessive downsizing.

2.   Get margins of flexibility from regular employees via work sharing, variable hours for core part-timers, work year contracts and voluntarily reduced work options.

3.   Use full-time equivalents instead of head counts to measure employment.

4.   Check whether the number of contingent workers has become larger than necessary.

5.   Smooth out fluctuations in the workload.

Use incentives and benefits:

1.   Link contingent worker's pay to performance.

2.   Offer regular employment as an incentive.

3.   Pay equitable — if not equal wages, offer benefits.

Look at quality and administration:

1.   Improve recruiting, selection and training of contingent workers.

2.   Use contingent staff only if they can do the work better or cheaper than your employees.

3.   Identify how your vendors recruit and retain their employees. How are their employees screened and tested?

4.   Substitute capital for labor by eliminating workers for technology.

Consider training costs:

1.   Hire already trained workers.

2.   Clearly define skills and experience.

3.   Simplify jobs.[70]

And what about the vendor's employees? How should they be managed? The SHRM foundation devotes an entire chapter to "Managing the Contingent Work Force" in its 1995 book, *The Contingent Worker, A Human Resource Perspective*. According to Gilmore McKie (a human resource generalist with both national

---

70. Excerpted by permission of the publisher, from *Managing Contingent Workers: How to Reap the Benefits and Reduce the Risks* by Stanley D. Nollen, et al © 1996 AMACOM, a division of American Management Association. All rights reserved.

and international experience as a vice president and director for Fortune 100 and 500 firms and listed in *Who's Who in America*) and co-author Lawrence Lipsett, Ed.D. (a consulting industrial psychologist, specializing in personnel selection and career development and author of 45 articles involving human resource management, industrial psychology, etc.), "managing contingent workers involves many of the same issues involved in managing regular workers."[71]

Scheduling issues must be addressed before workers begin. McKie and Lipsett recommend that these questions be asked: "How long will they be needed? What hours will they be needed? Can job sharing be arranged? What provisions are made for emergencies, like illness? Who is responsible for scheduling?"[72] In addition, are there enough work stations? How will working hours fit with production?

Karen Meyer-Bentley of Colorbok says that contingent workers should be managed in the same way as regular workers. When approached by her vendor to bring in on-site coordinators to oversee their temporaries, she politely declined, declaring that such posturing made temporaries feel they were not part of the team.[73]

Colorbok works hard to show its temporary workers that they are an integral part of the organization. With the exception of legally required differences, temporary employees receive "every single thing regular full-time workers do," says Meyer-Bentley. Prior to doing this, Meyer-Bentley states that contingent workers segregated themselves, and efficiency and morale suffered.[74]

Colorbok, a Dexter, Michigan-based leading manufacturer of gifts, stationary, and toys for children, also utilizes independent designers to provide freelance designs. Using a variety of designers

---

71. Reprinted with the permission of The Society of Human Resource Management Foundation from *The Contingent Worker: A Human Resources Perspective* by Gordon McKie and Laurence Lipsett, 1995.
72. Ibid

allows Colorbok the luxury of paying by design for the style, format, and image they want.

"While one designer might be really great at designing for the spring season, another might be better equipped at designing for children. Outsourcing gives us all the options, all the time," says Meyer-Bentley.[75]

Maxine Richmond of ADECCO reminds us to:

1. Know what makes a contingent worker tick.
    a. Why did the contingent worker choose this line of work — was it for intellectual need, variety, life style issues, family, pursuit of education?
2. Make the worker a part of your team.
    a. Specify objectives and expected results. Make sure directives are understood.
    b. Introduce and explain the worker's role to the rest of the team.
    c. Add help/support as necessary.
3. Evaluate and offer feedback.
    a. Tell them what you like about their work.
    b. Be positive and direct about how they can improve.[76]

Organizations should be particularly sensitive to the human side of outsourcing. Perceived threats or feelings of insecurity, wage differentials, reluctance to share information, reduction in hours worked or overtime pay for regular employees, and lack of incentives for the contingent worker all set the stage for *teamwork* failure when trying to integrate employees and contracted workers.[77]

It is critical to communicate with all of the parties involved in an up-front and honest manner. Full-time workers are more likely to co-operate if they are assured that their jobs are not threatened. Contingent workers have more positive attitudes if they have genuine opportunities for full-time employment — but don't expect it.[78]

Effective and early orientation for outsourcing vendors and their workers, using existing employee resources to plan and present goals and information, or provide training can often result in not only more qualified contracted labor but the early stages of teamwork.

Periods of transition, such as orientation, temporary to permanent status, downsizing, phase-ins, partial retirement, and negotiated part-time can be very vulnerable times for everyone and must be planned and orchestrated very carefully.

Making the worker part of the team is not without some risk. Outsourcing users that follow the Internal Revenue Service 20-Factor Test (used to determine span of control), can find it difficult to interpret at best.

In a *Nation's Business* article, "Contract Workers: A Risky Business," author Joan Szabo states that it is clear that organizations need to take extra steps to insure IRS compliance; steps that can be difficult because of tax law. While her article cites cases where organizations clearly distinguished employees from independent contractors, companies were required to pay penalties, interest, and attorney fees before they won their case in district court.[79]

Joan Stern, who has spent her entire career with the Wage and Hour Division of the U.S. Department of Labor as an investigator in Brooklyn, New York, Washington D.C., and now Lansing, Michigan, says that the very thought of investigating worker misclassification as it relates to independent contractors sets her hair on end. "You wouldn't believe the reasons that organizations give us to defend their belief that employees are independent contractors," says Stern.[80]

"We've been told that the contractors rent desks, office equipment, PC's, and software from them or that the independent contractor elected to use the company's forms or supplies. They've asked us 'Why are you here? I'm good to my people. We're just like a family,' or 'Why didn't we know about this before we started our business or contracted for an independent?' " says Stern.[81]

Chapter 8 is designed to assist business professionals in learning to identify the myriad legal issues that surround outsourcing.

On a daily basis, statutes are enacted and reach sunset, regulations are amended, litigated and terminated, and court opinions issued and overruled. As a result, no print publication is up-to-date. In addition, both state and federal law apply or cross paths in most employment issues, adding to the complexity. This chapter is intended to generally acquaint the reader with the scope of legal issues surrounding outsourcing; it cannot claim to be as current as this morning's headlines.

As with the rest of this book, this chapter is not intended in any manner to offer legal or other expert advice. If legal or other expert advice is required, those services should be sought from appropriate professionals.

Readers are encouraged to consider as an additional resource a publication of the Michigan Chamber of Commerce, *A Michigan Employer's Guide to Flexible Staffing*, by Miller, Canfield, Paddock and Stone, P.L.L.C. Excerpts and paraphrasing of that volume, with the permission of the publisher, constitute a considerable portion of this chapter.

Readers are also encouraged to contact their state chambers of commerce for reference and referral to applicable state labor and employment laws and regulations.

8.

Legal Issues

BACKGROUND

ACCORDING TO THE BUREAU OF LABOR STATISTICS, THE NUMBER OF persons performing as outsourcers has increased from 417,000 in 1982 to more than 1.4 million in 1992, a nearly 250% increase in just ten years. In the next decade, job growth in the industry is expected to increase 1.5 times faster than any other industry.[82]

Given this trend, legal issues affecting outsourcers are drawing attention from employers, labor unions, and the U.S. government.[83] In the SHRM publication, *Workplace Visions*, it is noted that:

> Employers can expect renewed federal and Congressional interest in the welfare of contingent workers over the next several years. The Internal Revenue Service announced plans in August 1995 to improve the worker-classification system for independent contractors. The Congress, Senator

---

82. Reprinted with the permission of The Michigan Chamber of Commerce

Christopher Bond (R-Mo) and eight other Senators...co-sponsored the Independent Contractor Tax Simplification Act of 1996 (S.1610). In addition, the Commission on the Future of Worker-Management Relations, appointed by Secretary of Labor Robert Reich and the late Secretary of Commerce Ron Brown, has identified upgrading the economic status of contingent workers as one of its 10 goals for the 21st century work place.[84]

With outsourcing, employers are *experimenting* with core work forces and are exposing themselves to new issues in the law that they may not readily recognize (i.e., copyright law).

The AFL-CIO is lobbying for revisions to existing labor laws (which include redefining the terms "employee" and "employer").[85]

Washington watches intently for evasive behavior from employers who would intentionally classify employees as independent contractors to avoid paying taxes or benefits. As a check and balance, the IRS has created special task forces to conduct employment audits of small and medium-size employers who consistently rely on independent contractors.[86]

Organizations will be better equipped to determine if outsourcing can fill their needs if they understand the legal issues that impact outsourcing. Let's examine a few:

COMMON LAW TEST

The common law test is applied by the courts in tort cases involv-

from *A Michigan Employer's Guide to Flexible Staffing* by Miller, Canfield, Paddock & Stone, 1994.

83. Ibid.

85-105. Ibid

ing the conduct of an employee during the course and within the scope of employment.

In such cases, the courts will look to more than just the control issue and review such factors as:

1. Is the worker performing services generally regarded by the general public as a business or occupation performed without supervision;

2. Is the worker licensed, incorporated or a registered business;

3. Does this work require high level skills, training, or experience and did the worker have it prior to this assignment;

4. What tools are provided and who supplies them;

5. Who determines the time parameters;

6. Did all parties intend and/or understand that this was to be an independent contractor relationship.[87]

Liabilities for tortious conduct committed by an independent contractor will generally not apply to the user contracting with the independent contractor unless:

1. The work performed is dangerous;

2. The work performed was not inspected by the contracting user;

3. The contracting user was negligent in selection of the independent contractor;

4. The contracting user has notice of potential tortious conduct and fails to address/prevent it; or

5. The contracting user requires/supervises or directs the actions which result in the alleged injury.[88]

ECONOMIC REALITY TEST

The economic reality test is utilized for "Remedial Statutes," such as those state laws that provide for workers' compensation, wages and hours, and unemployment benefits, and the Federal Fair Labor Standards Act.

As noted in Miller et al., "...the relevant factors to be considered under this test are (1) control of a worker's duties, (2) the payment of wages, (3) the right to hire, fire and discipline, and (4) the performance of the duties as an integral part of the employer's business towards the accomplishment of a common goal."[89]

The economic reality test is also used by courts to determine employment status under federal and state civil rights acts.[90]

EMPLOYMENT DISCRIMINATION STATUTES

In interpreting and applying employment discrimination laws, some courts have stated that the right and extent of control over the worker is the primary factor. Thus, while "outsourced workers" are not employees in a conventional sense, they may still be found by the courts to be subject to control by an outsourcing user entity in some aspects of their compensation, terms, and conditions and thus found to be employees.[91]

IMMIGRATION REFORM AND CONTROL ACT

As stated by Miller et al., the 1986 Immigration Reform and Control Act (IRCA) requires employers with three or more employees to verify that employees are legally entitled to work in the United States and prohibits employment discrimination based on national origin or citizenship status. While IRCA imposes penalties for knowingly hiring unauthorized aliens (as well as paperwork violations relative to the I-9 form), penalties do not apply to independent contractors.[92]

The Immigration and Naturalization Service applies both factors similar to the common law test in its determination of employment status (8 CFR § 274a. 1(j)).[93]

Under IRCA regulations, "...in the case of an independent contractor or contract labor or services, the term employer shall mean the independent contractor or contractor and not the person or entity using the contract labor" (8 CFR § 274a. 1(g)).[94]

INTELLECTUAL PROPERTY: PATENTS

"In general, if the employee is the inventor, the employee owns the patent rights, however, if the employee is hired to invent or solve problems," as noted by Miller et al., then the employee may have a duty to assign rights to the contracting user.[95]

If the invention is outside the general function of the employment but, as stated in Miller et al., "utilizes the employer's time, materials and/or machines, then the invention is still owned by the employee but may be subject to a 'shop right' on the part of the employer to practice the invention."[96]

IRS 20-FACTORS TEST AND RELATED COMPLIANCE

To ensure that workers are classified properly for federal tax reporting and payment purposes (and taxes fall to the appropriate parties), organizations follow the guidelines of the Internal Revenue Service. The IRS applies a 20-factors test derived from common law utilizing span of control as IRS criteria, (the more control, the greater the chance that the worker is an employee). This test asks outsourcing users to examine the following factors:

1. **Instructions.** Is the worker required to comply with other persons' instructions about when, where, and how he or she is to work?

2. **Training.** Is the worker required to work with an experienced worker, correspond with the worker or required to attend meetings?

3. **Integration.** How integrated is the worker's service into the business?

4. **Services Rendered Personally.** Must the service be rendered personally by the worker?

5. **Hiring, Supervising, and Paying Assistants.** Who is responsible for hiring, supervising, and paying assistants — the contracting user or the worker?

6. **Continuing Relationship.** Is the relationship continuous?

7. **Set Hours of Work.** Who establishes the hours of work — the worker or the contracting user?

8. **Full-time Required.** Must the worker devote substantially full-time hours to the contracting user?

9. **Doing Work on Employer's Premises.** Must the work be done on the contracting user's premises or can it be done elsewhere?

10. **Order or Sequence Set.** Is the worker free to follow his/her own pattern of work or required to follow established routines, schedules, order, or sequence of contracting user?

11. **Oral or Written Reports.** Is the worker required to submit regular or written reports to the contracting user?

12. **Payment by Hour, Week, Month.** Is payment by the hour, week, month, or project, job task, and/or commission?

13. **Payment of Business and/or Travel Expenses.** Does the contracting user ordinarily pay the worker's business and/or travel expenses?

14. **Furnishing of Tools and Materials.** Who furnishes significant tools, materials, and other equipment?

15. **Significant Investment.** Does the worker invest and use facilities and/or equipment that are not typically maintained by the outsourcing user's employees?

16. **Realization of Profit or Loss.** Is the worker subject to a real risk of economic loss due to significant investments or a bona fide liability for expenses, such as salary payments to unrelated workers?

17. **Working for More Than One Firm at a Time.** Does the worker perform more than de minimis services for a multiple of unrelated persons or firms at the same time.

18. **Making Services Available to General Public.** Does the worker offer services through advertising, business cards, referral services, etc.?

19. **Right to Discharge.** Does the contracting user retain the right to discharge the worker or do contract specifications include contract expiration or contract termination for cause language?

20. **Right to Terminate.** Does the worker have the right to end his or her relationship with the contracting user at any time he or she wishes without incurring liability?

Employers found guilty of intentional misclassification may be assessed significant penalties. Unintentional misclassification receive lesser penalties (26 USC §§ 3102, 3301, 3402, and 3509).

The IRS may also impose interest and civil penalties for failures, for example, to properly withhold or failing to pay taxes (26 USC §§ 6601, 6651, 6656, and 6662).

[For a more extensive description of the IRS 20-Factor Test, please see Appendix D, page 129.]

LIABILITY ISSUES (JOINT)

Because employers generally supervise the temporary/leased workers as they relate to work assignments, time schedules, processes, working conditions, and other terms and conditions, liability as a joint (or second) employer may apply.

Title VII of the Civil Rights Act of 1984
Federal law prohibits discrimination in employment by covered employers because of "race, color, religion, sex, or national origin." Organizations should also refer to state laws for weight, height, marital status, and other protected classes (42 USC § 2000 e).

Age Discrimination in Employment Act
Covered employers are prohibited from discriminating against persons age forty years or over (29 USC § 623).

Americans with Disabilities Act
For covered employers, this act prohibits practices that would discriminate against "qualified" disabled individuals in all employment

practices. It restricts interviewing questions to performance/job specific qualifications and requires accommodation unless this creates an undue hardship for the employer.

The act also requires identification of essential job functions, provides small business tax incentives, and requires handicap access to building structures (42 USC § 12101 et seq.).

Family and Medical Leave Act of 1993 (FMLA)

This act covers all employers with at least fifty employees within 75 miles of the work site. Employees are covered if employed by the employer for at least twelve months and worked for the employer for at least 1,250 hours during the preceding twelve months.

Employees are entitled to leaves of up to twelve weeks for their own serious health condition or to care for a child, spouse, or parent. During the absence, the employee is entitled to receive health benefits on the same terms as if an active employee. Upon return from FMLA leave, the employee must be able to resume the same or equivalent position (29 USCA § 2601 et seq.).

Wage and Hour Laws

See page 90.

National Labor Relations Act

Also referred to as the Wagner Act or the Magna Carta of labor, it encourages collective bargaining and:

1. Establishes workers' rights to organize;

2. Defines unfair labor practices; and

3. Establishes the National Labor Relations Board to enforce rules (29 USC 151 et seq.).

Workers Compensation

Most states offer exclusive remedy provisions for on-the-job death or disability of employees. Independent contractors may not be limited by such statutes and may, therefore, seek civil action against the party contracting for their services. The issue for the contracting party becomes one of whether the person is an employee or an independent contractor under relevant statutory definitions and the relevant tests to be applied.

LIABILITY ISSUES (SEPARATE)

Occupational Safety and Health

Under the Occupational Safety and Health Act (OSHA), the client employer, not the staffing company, is primarily liable for violations of OSHA Standards (29 USC § 651).[97]

Immigration Reform and Control Act

"...in the case of an independent contractor or contract labor or services, the term employer shall mean the independent contractor or contractor and not the person or entity using the contract labor" (8 CFR § 274a.1(g)).[98]

Payroll Taxes

The Internal Revenue Code provides that:

> ...[if] the person for whom the individual performs or performed the services does not have control of the payment of the wages for such services, the term employer . . . means the person having control of the payment of such wages (26 USC § 3401(d)(1)).

PENSION AND OTHER BENEFITS

There is no law that requires any employer to provide benefits to leased employees. However, Internal Revenue Code, Section 414 (n) was passed in 1982 as part of the Tax Equity and Fiscal Responsibility Act (TEFRA), and is often referred to as the "employee leasing law" (29 USC § 414(n))[99]. This code section provides regulation of the treatment of leased employees with regard to benefit programs.

This section is a result of employee leasing arrangements where employees were terminated and leased back through leasing companies to avoid the benefits requirements of Section 401 of the Employee Retirement Income Security Act of 1974 (ERISA) (29 USC § 1001 et seq.), as well as Internal Revenue Code coverage tests. These actions resulted in pension and other benefits being provided to only higher-level employees and disregarding others.[100]

For benefit plan purposes, Section 414(n) defines a "leased employee" as any person not an employee of the client employer but who performs services for such employer pursuant to an agreement between a staffing company and a client employer on a "substantially full-time basis" for a period of at least one year where such services are the same as those historically performed by regular employees (IRC § 414(n) (2)).[101]

COPYRIGHTS

"In general, the author is the copyright owner. However, if the author is an employee and work is prepared by the employee within the scope of his/her employment, then the employer is deemed to be the author."[102] An independent contractor is the owner of the copyright in a work created by the contractor unless special conditions are met.

TRADE SECRETS

By establishing and enforcing policies which insure that protectable information will be kept confidential, the employer is deemed to own all proprietary and confidential information developed in the business.

When possible, contracting users create independent contractor agreements that clearly define responsibilities, liabilities and ownership. This cannot be done without a clear understanding of the law.

UNEMPLOYMENT COMPENSATION

In some states, employers are only required to make contributions to their unemployment insurance fund based on the payment of taxable wages. Claims could, however, arise where a person who has been working as an independent contractor files a claim for unemployment benefits. If the contracting user contests, the applicable state commission can investigate the user's conduct and issue a determination.

While states govern their own criteria, employment may be defined as broadly as service performed for remuneration or under any contract of hire, written or oral, express or implied.[103]

WAGE AND HOUR LAWS

As noted by Miller et al., "The economic reality test is used to determine whether a worker is an employee for purposes of the Fair Labor Standards Act..." (29 USC § 203 et seq.).[104]

On a federal level, the law regulates, determines, and enforces minimum wage and minimum wage exceptions, training wage, overtime issues, definition of the work week, travel pay, wage conditions, investigations, inspections, records, homework regulations, child labor provisions, penalties and injunctions (29 USC § 201 et seq.).

WORKERS ADJUSTMENT AND RETRAINING NOTIFICATION ACT (WARN)

In WARN, it appears that covered employers are under no obligation to give sixty days written notice to independent contractors affected by plant closings or layoffs (29 USC § 2101 et seq.), as noted by Miller et al.[105]

9.

Union Issues

Outsourcing has become the craze among American firms.[106]

GM strikes reveal worker anxiety heading into talks.[107]

STATEMENTS LIKE THESE CONTINUE TO HAUNT UNIONS, MANAGEment, and the American worker.

Industry watchers such as Mark Erenburg, director of the Labor-Management Relations Center at Cleveland State University feels that, "When job security is the prime concern, then any threat to your job is a threat to your way of life."[108]

THE DELPHI STORY - THE NEED FOR TECHNOLOGY

Job security was the number one strike issue at General Motors and the Delphi parts factories in Dayton, Ohio, during the spring of 1996. Was the company's argument valid that a reduction of the work force was needed because improved manufacturing processes meant fewer people were needed to produce components and systems? Or was the real issue that General Motors had squeezed out union employees in its attempt to lower costs by outsourcing to independents?

Why would General Motors buy parts from the Robert Bosch Company in Charleston, South Carolina, rather than from Delphi (which it owns)? It was the need for technology that prompted General Motors' action. This step propelled the company into a strike that made national headlines and impacted the Big Three American auto companies and workers for years to come.

IT'S ALSO A MATTER OF ECONOMICS

Economists say that outsourcing has had a negative effect on American wages. In the past, organizations wishing to remain union-free were forced to pay union equivalent or higher wages and benefits.

In today's global market economy, organizations are rushing to outsourcing opportunities that will reduce costs and add value. Smaller non-union suppliers can now offer faster, flexible options and are willing to compete with each other for market share. They operate for less and can afford to contract for less. This downward trend in wages has resulted in rank and file workers being forced to accept wage concessions or face work force reductions.

Once an industry begins to enjoy the benefits of outsourcing, they are reluctant to give them up and will use whatever legal means possible to insure those benefits, while still protecting the integrity of their product.

What does this mean for the Big Three auto companies who once made their own parts but now outsource them to lower-wage, non-union suppliers? It means closed factories and work force reductions.

When General Motors wants to expand outsourcing and tells the United Auto Workers they will not guarantee jobs, and competitor Ford Motor Company allows only *traditional* outsourcing (as a buffer for fluctuations in business), who knows how this tug-of-war will end?[109]

The UAW is not alone in its fight for job security. Over 6,700 machinists at McDonnell-Douglas Corporation in St. Louis were on strike for months seeking a promise that their jobs would not be eliminated during the next several years. "But McDonnell-Douglas managers say no reasonable labor contract can guarantee workers jobs in an era when companies must constantly look for ways to cut costs and become more efficient if they want to stay in business."[110]

Unions are resisting in more ways than just standing their ground on wage cuts or outsourcing. The labor movement continues to lobby for government help, such as the ability to organize smaller organizations or walking away from national health insurance benefits because of the advantages non-union firms would enjoy.

What do the unions want with respect to outsourcing? One topic discussed repeatedly by the UAW in talks with both Ford and General Motors during the 1996 contract negotiations, was the "possibility of expanding the union's membership by pushing parts makers to allow their work forces to be unionized... Laws covering fair-labor practices prohibit the union and any auto makers from discriminating against another company because of its union status," said the *Wall Street Journal*. All parties could run into roadblocks regarding this issue.[111]

The two sides also discussed ways to encourage automakers to make more of their own parts, "thus preserving jobs that might otherwise go to outside nonunion suppliers. Specifically, if Ford acquired new parts businesses, it would be able to pay the new workers less than its assembly workers. In return, the automakers would agree to minimum employment levels at its assembly plants."[112]

Perhaps the loudest message has come from the new AFL-CIO president, John L. Sweeney, whose tenet is aggressive organizing.

Sweeney nearly doubled the size of his Service Employees International Union (SEIU) by putting a third of the Union's budget into organizing efforts. He now plans to do the same at the AFL-CIO.

Across the country, organized labor is conducting door-to-door organizing, television blitzes, hardball political campaigns, and intimidation tactics that include such techniques as "salting". Salting involves sending numerous, sometimes hundreds, of union members to a contractor's office to apply for employment. If or when applicants are turned away, the applicant's union files a charge of discrimination with the National Labor Relations Board (NLRB). Legal fees can cost from $3,000 to $15,000.[113]

In spite of the desire of a small business to hang tough, the union's goal of forcing the business to accept the union or go out of business is clear.

Union organizing strategies include the Building Trades Project, whose efforts in Las Vegas could impact small business nationally. This project includes confrontations with small, family-owned, non-union construction companies and what John L. Sweeney refers to as "heavy artillery" positions to go all over the country.[114] It includes accusations of NLRB violations, crowds of union workers on or near non-union sites, aggressive and often hostile behavior and other unpleasant and unsettling activities that could reflect negatively on a small business owner.

As if the unions were not busy enough, the NLRB in Washington, D.C. is signaling a change of national employment policy that may strike a lethal blow to an entire industry and its employees. The board is considering hearing cases that may force temporary workers into unions against their will. If the board rules that the customer and client are joint employers — each must then bargain with the temporary employee.

As discussed previously, companies utilize temporaries to determine their performance, address flexible work arrangements, and cut costs, benefits, or legal obligations. Should the union prevail at these hearings, union membership will increase and the desire to use temporary employees may be reduced.

Human resource professionals are taking heed of these and other developments in the labor market. Much like Paul Revere on his famous midnight ride, I turn to outsourcers with the following words of alarm... "The unions are coming, the unions are coming!"

These indicators should serve as a warning to outsourcers of all sizes to examine their policies, pay structures, employee attitudes, and working conditions or face successful organizing efforts and the costly consequences that often follow.

10.

Opinions, Forecasts, and Projections

OUTSOURCING IS A SMART STRATEGY

WHAT DO OTHER RESEARCHERS, OUTSOURCERS, AND EDUCATORS SAY about outsourcing? Is it a smart strategy that will cut costs and improve profits?

According to *The Advisor*, a newsletter published by SHRM, "Outsourcing has become a major growth area in the economy as companies continue to increase their use of outside contractors to perform functions that require skills the companies lack, would cost too much to perform in-house or would divert attention from improving the firm's products or services."[115]

The Advisor also reported that "A group of owners of small, home-based businesses have informed the Senate Small Business Committee that their companies represent an important growth component in the economy..."[116]

Other experts cite:

"The organization man is setting out on his own — and setting in motion powerful new dynamics in economy, society and politics. As the information revolution reshapes the structure of the business world, the number of Americans who are self-employed or own their own business is steadily rising. Already, the number of self-employed Americans roughly equals or even exceeds the number of workers in unions," according to Ronald Brownstein of the *Ann Arbor News*.[117]

"To survive, U.S. industry must continue to outsource work to more proficient, lower-cost locations. 'Delocalization' strategies are essential as the pool of skilled labor deepens around the world," John Judis of *The New Republic* noted in quoting the *Journal of Business Strategy*.[118]

Indeed, strong growth is ahead for outsourcers, as virtually "every industry considers outsourcing to help cut costs," predicted John Verity of *Business Week*.[119]

"Gone are the days when a short-term job was something to be embarrassed about. In fact, they're likely to be the norm by the year 2000. 'Projections are that by the turn of the century, more than half of the work force will be employed in a 'temporary' job situation in one form or another,' according to New York City-based Lee Hecht Harrison's Jane Cerri, director of professional services," said Valerie Frazee of *Personnel Journal*.[120]

Frazee also added, "Workers are re-examining their relationships with their jobs. The downsizing and layoffs of the past few years have caused people to question their loyalty to a single employer and begin to understand that lifetime employment is a thing of the past."[121]

"Computer outsourcing — the farming out of data processing to a third-party company — has become one of the hottest business developments in corporate America," said Alice Lusk, contributor to *Working Woman* magazine.[122]

"Another unmistakable trend: Money is not going to build bigger staffs. In fact, the majority of corporations are downsizing their central design departments like crazy. It's all part of the great decentralization of the American corporation," theorized Bruce Nussbaum of *Business Week*.[123]

"It is quite clear that management can no longer be relied upon in the same way. Workers have become...more entrepreneurial, self-interested, and opportunistic. Individual self-direction reigns over group cooperation; independent, personal agendas take priority over compromise," said Audrey Freedman in the SHRM publication, *Human Resource Forecast 1996*.[124]

"Call it whatever you like — a non-traditional work force, a flexible work force, a low-fixed cost work force, a just-in-time work force — it's real, it's radical and it's being implemented right now in organizations across the country," said Seth Kerker of the International Quality and Productivity Center, which specializes in training seminars on flexible staffing and core business strategies.[125]

11.

What Needs Are Met With Outsourcing?

I̲T̲ I̲S̲ E̲S̲T̲I̲M̲A̲T̲E̲D̲ T̲H̲A̲T̲ "T̲E̲M̲P̲O̲R̲A̲R̲I̲E̲S̲, I̲N̲D̲E̲P̲E̲N̲D̲E̲N̲T̲ C̲O̲N̲T̲R̲A̲C̲T̲O̲R̲S̲, and consultants hired by organizations; temporaries hired through staffing companies; and on-call part-time workers" comprise from 5% to as high as 20% of all U.S. employees, according to Phaedra Brotherton, in her 1995 *HR Magazine* article, "Staff to Suit."[126]

According to the Bureau of Labor Statistics [see Table 3, page 104], as many as six million employees (4.9 % of the U.S. labor force) work in temporary jobs.

These estimates include almost any worker who believed he/she to be working in a temporary position when the 60,000 households were surveyed. Service industries received the highest score (54%); followed by wholesale and retail trades (12%); manufacturing (10.8%); construction (9.8%); transportation and public utilities

---

126. Reprinted with the permission of the publisher from "Staff to Suit" by Phaedra Brotherton from *HR Magazine*, published by the Society of Human Resource Management, Alexandria, VA, December 1995.

(4.2%); public administration (3.6%); agriculture, finance, insurance and real estate (2.6%); and mining (0.3%).

The occupational breakdown of the contingent work force showed that professional specialty received the highest percentage (20.6%); followed by administrative support (including clerical) (17.7%); service occupations (16.0%); operators, fabricators, and laborers (15.8%); precision production, craft, and repair (10.0%); executive administrative, and managerial (7.6%); sales occupations (6.4%); farming, forestry, and fishing (3.0%); and technical and related support (2.7%) [Table 4, see page 105].

Table 3
Industrial Breakdown of Contingent Work Force

INDUSTRY	CONT.	NON CONT.
Total, 16 years and over (thousands)	6,034	117,174
Percent	100.0	100.0
Agricultural	2.6	2.6
Mining	0.3	0.6
Construction	9.8	5.5
Manufacturing	10.8	17.1
Transportation and Public Utilities	4.2	7.2
Wholesale and Retail Trade	12.0	20.9
Finance, Insurance and Real Estate	2.6	6.7
Services	54.0	34.5
Public Administration	3.6	5.0

NOTE: Details for the above will not sum to totals due to rounding and other group entries not provided.

Source: Bureau of Labor Statistics, Bureau of National Affairs Inc., February 1995

Of the 19 vendors appearing in an advertising directory in the September 1993 issue of *The Personnel Journal,* 35% provided administrative services and 26% provided personnel staffing that included office, marketing, technical, light industrial, human resource management, data base design maintenance, business consultation, and more. Technical skills were provided by 13%, and 5.2% offered to manage the employment relationship.[127]

Numbers continue to support that routine laborious, seasonal, and difficult tasks are finding their way into the hands of outsourcers.

Table 4
Occupational Breakdown of Contingent Work Force

INDUSTRY	CONT.	NON CONT.
Total, 16 years and over (thousands)	6,034	117,174
Percent	100.0	100.0
Executive, administrative, and managerial	7.6	14.0
Professional specialty	20.6	14.6
Technicians and related support	2.7	3.2
Sales occupations	6.4	12.2
Administrative support, including clerical	17.7	15.0
Service occupations	16.0	13.4
Precision production, craft, and repair	10.0	10.8
Operators, fabricators, and laborers	15.8	14.2
Farming, forestry, and fishing	3.0	2.6

NOTE: Details for the above will not sum to totals due to rounding and other group entries not provided.

Source: Bureau of Labor Statistics, Bureau of National Affairs Inc., February 1995

12.

Outsource Wisely, Outsource Well

WHILE TODAY'S WORKPLACE OFFERS INCREASED TECHNOLOGY, expanded job knowledge, and team and quality concepts, the goals of corporate America continue to be pretty much the same as they always were — lower costs and increase the profit margin.

Outsourcing can lower your costs and increase your profits, but it is not without risk. If you want creative, productive, enthusiastic, and dependable workers, you must handle your outsourcing wisely.

To successfully outsource you must:

1. **Know what outsourcing really can and cannot offer.** Any time an organization secures workers who have little or no attachment to the company for which they work, it can lead to exposures. Whether they work, when they work, and how much they work can depend on the needs of the organization or the whim of the worker.

   Opting for an outside individual or firm to provide a service that is usually or previously performed in-house can cause morale problems if not properly handled. Outsourcing options can include:

- ❏ contingent workers
- ❏ leased employees
- ❏ independent contractors
- ❏ contracted technical workers
- ❏ outsourcing companies
- ❏ temporary/part-time workers
- ❏ seasonal workers
- ❏ co-ops/interns
- ❏ home-based workers
- ❏ retirees
- ❏ contract workers
- ❏ direct hires

Regardless of what they are called, they all need standards and direction.

Ask why your organization is considering outsourcing before you begin. The business community utilizes outsourcing for a wide array of reasons including:

- ❏ decentralization
- ❏ advancements in technology
- ❏ flexibility
- ❏ erratic and seasonal staffing needs
- ❏ concentration on core competencies
- ❏ adjustments to growth and/or decline stages
- ❏ shifts from fixed to variable costs
- ❏ to reduce costs
- ❏ to add value
- ❏ specialty products and services
- ❏ time and delivery improvements

- ❏ to reduce complexity issues
- ❏ provide less opportunity for failure
- ❏ enhanced products and services are transparent to customers
- ❏ reduced liability

2. **Be creative—look for new opportunites.** While service organizations represent 54% of outsourcing, wholesale and retail services 12%, manufacturing 10.8%, and construction 9.8%, there remains a wide variety of other niche businesses to support you. Contact your local chamber of commerce for new members and new outsourcing opportunities.

    Professional speciality (20.6%), administrative support (17.7%), and operators, fabricators, and laborers (15.8%) represent the majority of the outsourcing occupations. These outsourcers may have worked on accounts tougher or more progressive than yours and have a great deal to offer.

3. **Be prepared for a new-generation worker.** Contractors are entrepreneurial, self-interested, and opportunistic. They are self-directed and have little or no attachment to the company at which they work. They desire flexibility, want to save the world, and would like to subsidize or increase their incomes.

    The majority of them are Generation X workers that fall between the ages of 20 and 34 years old. They are almost evenly split male to female. Over 80% are white. Almost 60% have completed high school or beyond and 27% are college graduates. They feel the rush, they crave the challenge, they go straight for the target!

4. **Stay focused.** Shifting work outside allows organizations to:

    ❑ concentrate on core competencies
    ❑ achieve higher quality
    ❑ experience cost and time savings
    ❑ reduce/eliminate liability issues (such as workers compensation and unemployment)
    ❑ secure advancements in technology
    ❑ expand the intellectual pool
    ❑ eliminate complex functions internally, and
    ❑ improve products and services

    To accomplish these goals, organizations need to focus on their role and that of the outsourcer.

5. **Know the negative effects of outsourcing.** For the organization, knowing the negative effects will help you avoid them. Negative effects include:

    ❑ lack of knowledge about the company or its culture
    ❑ high turnover
    ❑ lack of/or poor communication
    ❑ outsourcers too task oriented
    ❑ costs and assignments too hard to measure
    ❑ lack of relationships
    ❑ loss of control or supervision
    ❑ vendor complacency
    ❑ inflation over time
    ❑ a perceived threat to existing workers
    ❑ stress
    ❑ loss of time and error ratios

    Quality orientations, well-designed contracts, real partnering relationships, and ongoing communication are a must!

For the outsourcer, negative effects may include:

- ❏ multiple tasks/projects
- ❏ work imbalance/lack of security
- ❏ daily testing
- ❏ irregular or poorly defined schedules
- ❏ fast-paced/stressful environment
- ❏ payments that are withheld, delinquent, or difficult to collect
- ❏ tax and benefit costs must be paid by the outsourcer

6. **Take care of your outsourcing partner(s).** If you take good care of your outsourcer, your outsourcer will take good care of you.

    Managing the contingent work force requires the same planning, scheduling, and leadership capabilities as when managing an organization's regular work force. The organization must:

    - ❏ conduct orientations
    - ❏ get to know the worker
    - ❏ make the worker part of the team
    - ❏ draw on the worker's expertise
    - ❏ offer feedback
    - ❏ make the worker aware of their status
    - ❏ maintain excellent communication with all workers

7. **Plan in advance.** Consider the following factors before making and implementing an outsourcing decision:

    - ❏ set clear goals
    - ❏ take long and short-term perspectives
    - ❏ determine who and what will be controlled
    - ❏ define how company culture will support outsourcing
    - ❏ make centralized/decentralized decisions

❏ focus on business, not technical decisions

❏ define your plan and then announce it

❏ decide how/who will manage the relationship with outsourcers

❏ create ownership at the business level

❏ get advice from pioneers

Support decisions to outsource by checking for:

❏ competitive advantage

❏ support of organization needs, strategies, objectives, core competencies, and philosophies

❏ in-house costs now and into the future

❏ outsourcing costs now and into the future

❏ better service, improved technology

❏ delivery dates

❏ customizing options

❏ quality

8. **Control your cost.** While there is no question that cost savings play a major role in an organization's decision to outsource, evidence also points to drops in productivity, morale, increased training costs, employee turnover, agency, and administrative fees.

Organizations can balance the effect on cost, customers and the organization by: setting benchmarks based on current internal costs and quality levels; addressing the meaning of performance standards; determining specialized time or money investments; putting safeguards in place to prevent unfair increases; making services tangible by requiring reports, letters, charts; and including opt-out language for non-compliance or performance-based compensation arrangements.

Costs of contingent staffing can also be controlled by: accurate contingent staff sizing; incentives and benefits that fit the job; improved recruiting, selection and training of contingent workers; substituting capital for labor.

9. **Prepare for external conflicts.**

Legal Issues

Legal issues involving outsourcing are drawing attention from employers, labor unions, and the U.S. government. Organizations should understand the laws and the legal risks associated with outsourcing.

Worker classification issues can be addressed by applying the IRS 20 Factor Test; the common law test; and/or (3) the economic reality test.

Outsourcing generally exempts organizations from contributing to unemployment compensation or workers compensation but won't prevent workers from seeking civil action.

Employment discrimination statutes consider control by an employer entity and utilize the economic reality test to determine employment status.

Independent contractors are exempt from the Worker Adjustment and Retraining Notification Act.

Typically independent contractors are not eligible to receive overtime, minimum wage, or equal pay from the outsourcing user. The exceptions include economic reality tests that determine if an independent contractor is really an employee.

The Immigration Reform and Control Act requires employers (not organizations that outsource), to verify that employees are legally entitled to work in the United States.

While there is no law that requires any employer to provide pension or retirement benefits to independent contractors, IRS Code, Section 414(n) requires coverage tests to ensure the comparable benefits requirement of Section 401 of ERISA.

Joint liabilities include: Title VII; ADA; FMLA; wage and hour laws; Migrant and Seasonal Workers Protection Act; and The National Labor Relations Act.

Under OSHA, the client employer (not the vendor) is primarily liable for violations of OSHA standards.

Payroll taxes are the responsibility of the person having control of the payment of wages.

If a worker was not hired to invent or solve problems and the worker is the inventor, the worker owns the patent rights.

Union Issues

Organizations would be well advised to consider union organizing efforts now and in the future. Concerns for job security and declining wage scales are getting front page attention and hefty budget considerations by government agencies and unions.

Read and conduct research, and know the when, where, why and how of your business. Environmental scanning that surveys the current position of top ten suppliers, Fortune 500 companies, and union forces can help determine whether outsourcing will save or cost you in the long run.

10.   **Listen to the pros.** Consultants, owners, employers, busi-

ness strategists, business professionals, academics, and employees all share the same projections. They agree that outsourcing is a major growth area, that workers are re-examining their jobs and becoming more independent, that short-term employment is becoming the norm, and that lifetime employment is a thing of the past.

While it is clear from the research that outsourcing offers some well-defined benefits, it is critical that organizations pay heed to the advice from outsourcing pioneers. Decisions to outsource, what to outsource, how to outsource, how much to outsource, when to outsource, and to whom can all have negative impacts on overall costs, productivity, and morale. Other factors to consider are strategies, objectives, contracts, timing, technology, philosophies, communication, measurements and standards, costs and quality, recruiting, selection, training, safety, and alternate services.

Efforts must be made to identify every possible variable such as additional charges, increased volumes, equipment upgrades, capacity and overtime, taxes and inflation issues, emergency actions, backup and/or disaster planning, ownership of materials, records, systems, etc.

Contracts should always spell out performance expectations, measures, tests, and audits. Warranties, liability insurance, and references should be a prerequisite to doing business.

Organizations need to treat contingent workers with the same respect and dignity that should be afforded regular employees. They need to assess and utilize their skills, knowledge, and abilities, make them part of the team, make sure they are always aware of their status, and communicate, communicate, communicate.

Evidence indicates that outside influences such as legal, union, or governmental issues have and will continue to have an impact on outsourcing. For the most part legal issues favor outsourcing options, however, pressure from unions and government entities are not only cause for alarm for outsourcers, but are already changing legislation that affects outsourcing.

Recommendations for Further Action

Just a few more words of advice. If after reading the preceding chapters you feel that outsourcing is for you, we encourage you to refer to the checklist below and its extended version provided in Appendix A [page 117]:

1. Why do you want to outsource?

2. What do you know about the outsourcer?

3. What are the costs and contract terms?

4. How will you manage contingent workers?

5. What are the legal/labor issues affecting your organization?

6. What impact will outsourcing have on your employees?

The use of outsourcing can be your organization's biggest problem or greatest solution. Attention to the resources provided in this book can make the difference between maintaining a competitive edge or failure.

Establish your company's success by integrating outsourcing today.

Appendix A

Outsourcing Checklist

1. **Why do you want to outsource?**
   - ❏ Decentralization efforts
   - ❏ Advancements in technology
   - ❏ Increased flexibility
   - ❏ Seasonal staffing needs
   - ❏ Concentration on core competencies
   - ❏ Adjustment to growth/decline stages
   - ❏ Shift from fixed to variable costs
   - ❏ Reduce costs
   - ❏ Add value
   - ❏ To enjoy specialty products and services
   - ❏ Save time
   - ❏ Improve delivery dates
   - ❏ Outsource complex issues
   - ❏ Reduce failure rates
   - ❏ Reduce liabilities
   - ❏ Improve quality
   - ❏ Expand the intellectual pool
   - ❏ Improve products and services

2. What do you know about the outsourcer?

- ❏ Does their organization's philosophy fit with ours?
- ❏ Are they interested in partnerships and strategic alliances or sales?
- ❏ Do their services provide for our organization's needs?
- ❏ Is their technology superior to ours and are they willing to upgrade as necessary?
- ❏ Are their client base requirements compatible or do they conflict with our organization's needs?
- ❏ What is their response time?
- ❏ Are they willing to work on an as-needed basis?
- ❏ Are they experts in their field?
- ❏ Are they specialists in their field?
- ❏ Do they represent our competition (if not, why not?)?
- ❏ Is this vendor certified, licensed, or incorporated?
- ❏ Is this vendor insured (property, product liability, errors and omissions, medical, life, workers compensation [obtain copies and/or ask for carrier's name and number])?
- ❏ Is the work customized or pre-packaged?
- ❏ Have they met quality standards for your industry (ISO, QS9000)?
- ❏ How are they charging for their work (hourly rate, package prices, session)?
- ❏ Who are their clients?
- ❏ How long have they been in business?

3. What are the costs and contract terms?

- ❏ What are our current in-house costs?
- ❏ What will our future in-house costs be?
- ❏ How much would outsourcing cost?
- ❏ How much will future outsourcing cost?
- ❏ How are inflation or unidentified cost areas covered?
- ❏ Are bench marks set on internal costs and quality levels?

❏ Are there additional money investments on your part?

❏ What security measures are included?

❏ What proprietary measures are addressed?

❏ Are delivery dates or schedules defined?

❏ Are goals, objectives, and assignments clearly defined?

❏ Who will supervise what?

❏ Who is responsible for testing, parallel programs, and record keeping?

❏ What performance standards have been set?

❏ What reports, letters, charts will you require?

❏ What are the terms and conditions of payment?

❏ Can the contract be divided (nibbled) into units or short-term arrangements, projects, or individual services with renewal options?

❏ Is opt-out language for non-compliance or performance-based compensation provided?

4. **How will you manage contingent workers?**

❏ Make the worker(s) aware of their status

❏ Conduct an orientation

❏ Know your worker(s) knowledge, skills, and abilities

❏ Make your worker(s) part of the team

❏ Offer feedback

❏ Maintain excellent communication

5. **What are the legal issues affecting your organization?**

❏ IRS 20-Factor Test (conduct)

❏ Common Law Test (conduct)

❏ Economic Reality Test (conduct)

❏ Will contractors be contracted to invent or solve problems? Who will hold patent/rights?

❏ Will contractors be hired to create intellectual property and who will own it?

6. What impact will outsourcing have on your employees?

- ❏ How will you notify existing employees of your outsourcing decision?

- ❏ What effect will it have on morale?

- ❏ What impact will it have on your organization's wage scales?

- ❏ Is union organizing, unrest, or failure to cooperate an issue?

- ❏ Will work force reductions occur?

- ❏ Will employees share in increased profits?

- ❏ Will outsourcing benefit workers by offering mentoring, or training options not currently available?

Appendix B

Resources

Trade Publications
A Michigan Employer's Guide to Flexible Staffing
Labor & Employment Relations Department
Miller, Canfield, Paddock and Stone
600 S. Walnut St., Lansing, MI 48933
(517) 371-2100

Business Plan Guide for Independent Consultants, Herman Holtz
New York: Wiley, 1994
Topics: Business consultants, consulting (vocational guidelines)

Chicken Soup for the Soul at Work, Jack Canfield
Deerfield Beach, Florida: Health Communications, 1996
Topics: Work (moral and ethical aspects), interpersonal relations, employees (conduct of life), spiritual life, inspiration (anecdotes)

Computing Strategies for Re-engineering Your Organization,
Cheryl Currid & Company
Rocklin, California: Prima Publishers, 1996
Topics: Organization change, information change, information storage and retrieval systems, computer networks, business enterprises and re-engineering

Consultants and Consulting Organization's Directory, 1996
Detroit, Michigan: Gale Research Co., 1996
Topics: Business consultant's directory and government consultant's
directory

Consulting for Organizational Change, Fritz Steele
Amherst, Massachusetts: University of Massachusetts Press, 1975
Topics: Business consulting, problem solving, organizational change

Consulting: The Complete Guide to a Profitable Career, Robert Kelley
New York: Scribner, 1986
Topic: Consultants

Consulting to Management, Larry Greiner and Robert Metzger
Englewood Cliffs, New Jersey: Prentice-Hall, 1983
Topic: Business consultants

Job Shift: How to Prosper in a Workplace Without Jobs, William Bridges
Reading, Massachusetts: Addison-Wesley Publishing Company, 1994
ISBN: 0-201-48933-3
Topics: Unemployment, occupations, career changes, and labor market

Making the Most of Management Consulting Services, Jerome Fuchs
New York: AMACOM, 1975
Topic: Business consultants

*Managing Contingent Workers - How to Reap the Benefits and Reduce the
Risks,* Stanley Nollen and Helen Axel
New York: AMACOM, 1995, ISBN: 0814402429

Marketing Your Consulting or Professional Services, David Karlson
Los Altos, California: Crisp Publishing, 1988
Topics: Consulting (marketing), professions (marketing)

New Policies for the Part-time and Contingent Work Force,
Virginia Durivage (Editor), M. E. Sharpe, 1992, ISBN: 1563241641

*Peterson's Internships, 1997: 40,000 Opportunities to Get an Edge in
Today's Competitive Job Market*
Princeton, New Jersey: Peterson's Guides, 1996
Topics: Occupational training, employment training, internship, voca-
tional guide

Profitable Consulting: Guiding America's Managers into the Next Century, Robert Metzger
Reading, Massachusetts: Addison-Wesley, 1989
Topics: Business consulting, industrial management

Start and Run a Profitable Consulting Business, Douglas Gray
Vancouver, Seattle: International Self-counsel Press, 1986
Topic: Consultants

The Computer Consultant's Guide, Janet Ruhl
New York: Wiley, 1994
Topics: Business consulting, electronic data processing consultants

The Consultant's Kit: Establishing and Operating Your Successful Consulting Business, Jeffrey Lant
Cambridge, Massachusetts: JLA Publications, 1981
Topics: Business consultants

The Contingent Worker, W. Gilmore McKie
Virginia: The Society of Human Resource Management, 1995
ISBN: 0939900688

The Entrepreneur and Small Business Problem Solver, William Cohen
New York: Wiley, 1990
Topics: Small business, entrepreneurship

The Federal Wage and Hour Laws, Brian Dixon
Virginia: SHRM, 1994, ISBN: 0-93900-66-1

Welcome to the World of Independent Contractors and other Contingent Workers, Nancy E. Soerg
ISBN: 0808001019

The World of the Worker: Labor in 21st Century America, James Green
Hill and Wang, 1980
Topics: Working class history, trade union history

Work Concepts for the Future, Patricia Schiff Estess
ISBN: 1-56052-387-5

Work Force Growth Trends, Schoenfeld & Associates Inc., 1977
ISBN: 1-878339-60-5

Work Force 2000: Work/Worker for the 21st Century, William Johnson and Arnold Packer, and contributed by Matthew Jaffee
Indianapolis (Washington, D.C.): Hudson Institute and U.S. Department of Labor, 1987
Topics: Work class forecasting, employment forecasting, 21st century forecasts, economic forecasting, U.S. economy

Legal Counsel
Michigan Employment Law & Regulation
Labor and Employment Law Section: Dykema Gossett
Michigan Chamber of Commerce
600 S. Walnut St., Lansing, MI 48933, (517) 371-2100

Miller, Canfield, Paddock and Stone, P.L.L.C.
150 W. Jefferson, Suite 2500, Detroit, MI 48226-4415
(313) 963-6420

Periodicals
HR Focus (0956660, ISSN 1059-6038) is published monthly by The American Management Association, P.O. Box 57969, Boulder, CO 80322-7969, (800) 759-8520 or (303) 447-9330.

HR Magazine on Human Resource Management (ISSN 1047-3149) is published monthly by the Society for Human Resource Management (formerly American Society for Personnel Administration), 606 N. Washington Street, Alexandria, Virginia 22314, (703) 548-3440. Members of the society receive the magazine as part of their annual dues.

Michigan Forward (USPS 000-692) is published monthly for members of the Michigan Chamber of Commerce, 600 S. Walnut Street, Lansing, MI 48933, (517) 371-2100. A one-year subscription is included in members' annual dues.

Workforce (formerly *Personnel Journal*) (ISSN 0031-5745) is published monthly by ACC Communications Inc., 245 Fisher Avenue, B-2, Costa Mesa, CA 92626

Appendix C

Method

APPROACH

The review of literature focused on identifying what kind of organizational needs were met by outsourcing; positive effects, negative effects and critical factors in determining decisions to outsource. Research concentrated on existing writings from periodicals, journals, and bulletins, as well as studies completed by professional associations and universities.

Of significant importance to this book were the materials provided by the Society of Human Resource Management (SHRM), and contemporaries within the field of human resource management.

While the data base for the analysis focused on reviewing outsourcing from the end-user perspective, it should be understood that selected literature was limited to nationally recognized experts, scholars, and other human resource related professionals who either actively practice in the field of human resources or more specifically provide an outsourcing service to others.

DATA GATHERING METHOD

In an effort to discover data, professional human resource associations such as the nationally recognized Society of Human Resource Management (SHRM), and the respected Human Resource Management of Mid-Michigan and Ann Arbor Area Personnel Association were approached for their assistance.

SHRM provided both statistical and research data.

Research focused on common themes for a survey of Michigan-based organizations to test the hypotheses offered by experts, needs being met, effects, and other critical factors such as legal and union issues.

DATA BASE SELECTED FOR ANALYSIS

Existing surveys conducted by the Society of Human Resource Management Foundation, Linkage Inc., Hewitt Associates, The Bureau of Labor Statistics, The Bureau of National Affairs Inc., and Personnel Journal offered excellent data resources for the secondary method of data collection for the following reasons:

1.   A wider geographical dispersion was available than would be practical for our purposes.

2.   The diversity of themes would not lend well to a common recipient response without some duplication of effort by respondents.

Research data concentrated on information that would address what kinds of organizations would utilize outsourcing; in what areas is it most prevalent; characteristic of outsource workers; why organizations use outsourcers, and how outsourcing benefits the employer.

Related literature was used as a guide and reviewed for consistency of issues. The primary data source was provided by creating a six-question outsourcing survey that included a combination of closed and free-form type questions. The respondents were asked to make a choice between alternatives (yes or no), or multiple answers. The final questions simply called for comments. No information was offered as a clue.

Senior level human resource/financial executives, directors, chief executive officers, and presidents were selected to participate in the outsourcing survey.

Participants represented a wide range of industries that included computer services, relocation, temporary/leasing, paternity testing, blow molding, rehabilitation, engineering, manufacturing, etc.

The size of the organizations varied substantially, ranging from 2 to 350 employees.

ANALYSIS OF DATA - CATEGORY/THEME AND VALIDITY

Data was divided into common themes based on subject availability of related literature and the existence of representative data. In keeping with study objectives, data was provided utilizing the following themes:

1.   What kind of organizations use outsourcing?
     Industrial breakdown
     Occupational breakdown
     Directory of providers

2.   What are the characteristics?
     Age
     Ethnicity
     Education

3.   Why do organizations outsource?

4.   Is outsourcing cost effective?

5.   What are the negative effects of outsourcing?

6.   Does organizational maturity play a role?

All data provided was published in the last ten years and was provided by experts in the field of human resources, finance, technology, and marketing.

MEANS OF DETERMINING THE VALIDITY OF THE COMMON THEMES AND LIMITATIONS OF THE METHOD

In an attempt to validate existing surveys, questionnaires were mailed to chief executive officers, directors, and human resource professionals that had sufficient knowledge and qualifications to answer questions regarding strategic planning, alternative processes, and corporate culture values. It should be understood that personal interviews may have allowed a degree of perception error and are often met with both time constraints for the participant as well as a lack of hard data that might lead to subjective, not objective responses.

It is important to note that it is difficult to provide controlled group studies in light of the ever-changing dynamics of the business community.

STATISTICAL VALIDITY

No attempt was made to draw any statistical inferences from this book.

Appendix D

IRS 20-FACTOR TEST

As an aid to determining whether an individual is an employee under the common law rules, twenty factors or elements have been identified as indicating whether sufficient control is present to establish an employer-employee relationship. The twenty factors have been developed based on an examination of cases and rulings considering whether an individual is an employee. The degree of importance of each factor varies, depending on the occupation and the factual context in which the services are performed. The twenty factors are designed only as guides for determining whether an individual is an employee; special scrutiny is required in applying the twenty factors to assure that formalistic aspects of an arrangement designed to achieve a particular status do not obscure the substance of the arrangement (that is, whether the person or persons for whom the services are performed exercise sufficient control over the individual for the individual to be classified as an employee). The twenty factors are described below:

> 1. **Instructions.** A worker who is required to comply with other persons' instructions about when, where, and how he or she is to work is ordinarily an employee. This control factor is present if the person or persons for whom the services are performed have the right to require compliance with instructions.

2. **Training.** Training a worker by requiring an experienced employee to work with the worker, by corresponding with the worker, by requiring the worker to attend meetings, or by using other methods, indicates that the person or persons for whom the services are performed want the services performed in a particular manner.

3. **Integration.** Integration of the worker's services into the business operations generally shows that the worker is subject to direction and control. When the success or continuation of a business depends to an appreciable degree upon the performance of certain services, the workers who perform those services must necessarily be subject to a certain amount of control by the owner of the business.

4. **Services Rendered Personally.** If the services must be rendered personally, presumably the person or persons for whom the services are performed are interested in the methods used to accomplish the work as well as in the results.

5. **Hiring, Supervising, and Paying Assistants.** If the person or persons for whom the services are performed hire, supervise, and pay assistants, that factor generally shows control over the workers on the job. However, if one worker hires, supervises, and pays the other assistants pursuant to a contract under which the worker agrees to provide materials and labor and under which the worker is responsible only for the attainment of a result, this factor indicates an independent contractor status.

6. **Continuing Relationship.** A continuing relationship between the worker and the person or persons for whom the services are performed indicates that an employer-

employee relationship exists. A continuing relationship may exist where work is performed at frequently recurring although irregular intervals.

7. **Set Hours of Work.** The establishment of set hours of work by the person or persons for whom the services are performed is a factor indicating control.

8. **Full-time Required.** If the worker must devote substantially full-time to the business of the person or persons for whom the services are performed, such person or persons have control over the amount of time the worker spends working and impliedly restrict the worker from doing other gainful work. An independent contractor, on the other hand, is free to work when and for whom he or she chooses.

9. **Doing Work on Employer's Premises.** If the work is performed on the premises of the person or persons for whom the services are performed, that factor suggests control over the worker, especially if the work could be done elsewhere. Work done off the premises of the person or persons receiving the services, such as at the office of the worker, indicates some freedom from control. However, this fact by itself does not mean that the worker is not an employee. The importance of this factor depends on the nature of the service involved and the extent to which an employer generally would require that employees perform such services on the employer's premises.

Control over the place of work is indicated when the person or persons for whom the services are performed have the right to compel the worker to travel a designated route, to canvass a territory within a certain time, or to work at specific places as required.

10. **Order or Sequence Set.** If a worker must perform services in the order or sequence set by the person or persons for whom the services are performed, that factor shows that the worker is not free to follow the worker's own pattern of work but must follow the established routines and schedules of the person or persons for whom the services are performed. Often, because of the nature of an occupation, the person or persons for whom the services are performed do not set the order of the services or set the order infrequently. It is sufficient to show control, however, if such person or persons retain the right to do so.

11. **Oral or Written Reports.** A requirement that the worker submit regular or written reports to the person or persons for whom the services are performed indicates a degree of control.

12. **Payment by Hour, Week, Month.** Payment by the hour, week, or month generally points to an employer-employee relationship, provided that this method of payment is not just a convenient way of paying a lump sum agreed upon as the cost of a job. Payment made by the job or on a straight commission generally indicates that the worker is an independent contractor.

13. **Payment of Business and/or Traveling Expenses.** If the person or persons for whom the services are performed ordinarily pay the worker's business and/or traveling expenses, the worker is ordinarily the employee. An employer, to be able to control expenses, generally retains the right to regulate and direct the worker's business activities.

14. **Furnishing of Tools and Materials.** The fact that the person or persons for whom the services are performed furnish significant tools, materials, and other equipment tends to show the existence of an employer-employee relationship.

15. **Significant Investment.** If the worker invests in facilities that are used by the worker in performing services and are not typically maintained by employees (such as the maintenance of an office rented at fair value from an unrelated party), that factor tends to indicate that the worker is an independent contractor. On the other hand, lack of investment in facilities indicates dependence on the person or persons for whom the services are performed for such facilities and, accordingly, the existence of an employer-employee relationship. Special scrutiny is required with respect to certain types of facilities, such as home offices.

16. **Realization of Profit or Loss.** A worker who can realize profit or suffer a loss as a result of the worker's services (in addition to the profit or loss ordinarily realized by employees) is generally an independent contractor, but the worker who cannot is an employee. For example, if the worker is subject to a real risk of economic loss due to significant investments or a bona fide liability for expenses, such as salary payments to unrelated employees, that factor indicates that the worker is an independent contractor. The risk that a worker will not receive payment for his or her services, however, is common to both independent contractors and employees and thus does not constitute a sufficient economic risk to support treatment as an independent contractor.

17. **Working for More Than One Firm at a Time.** If a

worker performs more than de minimis services for a multiple of unrelated persons or firms at the same time, that factor generally indicates that the worker is an independent contractor. However, a worker who performs services for more than one person may be an employee of each of the persons, especially where such persons are part of the same service arrangement.

18. Making Service Available to the General Public. The fact that a worker makes his or her services available to the general public on a regular and consistent basis indicates an independent contractor relationship.

19. Right to Discharge. The right to discharge a worker is a factor indicating that the worker is an employee and the person possessing the right is an employer. An employer exercises control through the threat of dismissal, which causes the worker to obey the employer's instructions. An independent contractor, on the other hand, cannot be fired so long as the independent contractor produces a result that meets the contract specifications.

20. Right to Terminate. If the worker has the right to end his or her relationship with the person for whom the services are performed at any time he or she wishes without incurring liability, that factor indicates an employer-employee relationship.

Endnotes

1. Peter Druker, *Managing for the Future, the 1990's and Beyond* (New York: Truman Talley Books/Dutton), 93.

2. John Naisbitt and Patricia Aburdene, *Megatrends 1000. Ten New Directions for the 1990's* (New York: Morrow, 1990), 11-298.

3. *Time Magazine*, n.d.

4. *Time Magazine*, 29 Mar. 1993.

5. McKie and Lipsett, 01-44.

6. Bruce Nussbaum, "Is In-house Design on the Way Out?", *Business Week*, 25 Sept. 1995, 130.

7. Jennifer Laabs, "Successful Outsourcing Depends on Critical Factors," *Personnel Journal*, Oct. 1993, 51-60.

8. Scott Slyfield, telephone interview by author, Mar. 1997.

9. Lynn Brenner, "Reengineering Human Resources. The Disappearing HR Department," *CFO*, Mar. 1996, 61-64.

10. Brenner, 61-64.

11. Thomas Stewart, *Fortune Magazine*, 15 Jan. 1996, 105-107.

12. John Cooper, "Human Resources - Your Ticket to Success," *Michigan Forward*, Michigan Chamber of Commerce, July 1996, 26-27.

13. Cooper, 26-27.

14. Louis Fried, *Managing Information Technology in Turbulent Times* (New York: Wiley-QED, 1995), 158.

15. Fried, 158.

16. John Verity, "They Make a Killing Minding Other People's Business," *Business Week*, 30 Nov. 1992, 96.

17. Joyce Stackhouse, telephone interview by author, Mar. 1997.

18. Stackhouse, Mar. 1997.

19. Dennis Berkey, telephone interview by author, Mar. 1997.

20. Verity, 96.

21. Dennis Keith, telephone interview by author, Mar. 1997.

22. Keith, Mar. 1997.

23. Gordon McKie and Laurence Lipsett, *The Contingent Worker. A Human Resources Perspective* (Virginia: SHRM, 1995), 01-44.

24. Barney Olmsted and Suzanne Smith, *Creating a Flexible Workplace*, (AMACOM, 1989).

25. Karen Meyer-Bentley, telephone interview by author, Mar. 1997.

26. Debra Iben, telephone interview by author, Mar. 1997.

27. Gillian Flynn, "Contingent Staffing Requires Serious Strategy," *Personnel Journal*, Apr. 1995, 50-58.

28. James Spee, "Addition by Subtraction - Outsourcing Strengthens Business Focus," *HR Magazine*, Mar. 1995, 38-43.

29. Flynn, 50-58.

30. Martin J. Jerick, telephone interview by author, Mar. 1997.

31. Jerick, Mar. 1997.

32. Suellen Parkes, telephone interview by author, Mar. 1997.

33. Parkes, Mar. 1997.

34. John Byrne, "Has Outsourcing Gone Too Far?" *Business Week*, 1 Apr. 1996, 26-28, 32-33.

35. Slyfield, Mar. 1997.

36. Slyfield, Mar. 1997.

37. Byrne, 26-28, 32-33.

38. Phaedra Brotherton, "Staff to Suit," *HR Magazine*, Dec. 1995, 50-55.

39. Verity, 96.

40. Suzanne Oliver, "Cut Costs, Add a Middleman," *Forbes*, 25 Apr. 1994, 135.

41. Jennifer Laabs, "Why HR Is Turning to Outsourcing," *Personnel Journal*, Sept. 1993, 92-103.

42. Martin Stark, telephone interview by author, Mar. 1997.

43. Diane Mitchell, telephone interview by author, Mar. 1997.

44. Scott Derthick, telephone interview by author, Mar. 1997.

45. Keith, Mar. 1997.

46. Hewitt Associates survey results appearing in Jennifer Laabs, "Why HR is Turning to Outsourcing." *Personnel Journal*, Sept. 1993.

47. Linkage Inc. survey results appearing in Philip Harkins et al., "Shining New Light on a Growing Trend." *HR Magazine*, Dec. 1995.

48. "Supplement on Temporary/Leased Employees," *Business & Legal Reports*, Feb. 1993.

49. John Kotter, *The New Rules - How to Succeed in Today's Post-Corporate World*, (New York: Free Press Publishing, 1995), 86-94.

50. Kotter, 86-94.

51. Kotter, 86-94.

52. Spee, 38-43.

53. Laabs, 92-103.

54. Hank Van Kampen, telephone interview by author, Mar. 1997.

55. Laabs, citing Towers Perrin study, 51-60

56. Laabs, 51-60.

57. Flynn, 50-58.

58. Flynn, 50-58.

59. Kerry Hannon, "The Tempting Life of a Professional Temp," *U.S. News & World Reports*, 1997 Career Guide, 28 Oct. 1996, 80-81.

60. Lee Phillion and John Brugger, "Contingent Workforce Encore: Retirees Give Top Performance as Temporaries," *HR Magazine*, Oct. 1994.

61. Amy Saltzman, "You, Inc.," *U.S. News & World Reports*, 1997 Career Guide, 28 Oct. 1996, 66-79.

62. Saltzman, 66-79.

63. Hannon, 80-81.

64. Kotter, 86-94.

65. Maxine Richmond, telephone interview by author, Mar. 1997.

66. Richmond, Mar. 1997.

67. Richmond, Mar. 1997.

68. Philip Harkins, Stephen Brown, and Russell Sullivan, "Shining New Light On a Growing Trend," *HR Magazine,* Dec. 1995, 75-79.

69. Spee, 38-43.

70. Stanley Nollen and Helen Axel, *Managing Contingent Workers. How to Reap the Benefits and Reduce the Risks* (New York: AMACOM, 1995) and National Association of Temporary and Staffing Services quoted in Phaedra Brotherton, "Staff to Suit." *HR Magazine,* Dec. 1995, 50-55.

71. McKie and Lipsett, 01-44.

72. McKie and Lipsett, 01-44.

73. Meyer-Bentley, Mar. 1997.

74. Meyer-Bentley, Mar. 1997.

75. Meyer-Bentley, Mar. 1997.

76. Richmond, Mar. 1997.

77. Shari Caudron, "Contingent Work Force Spurs HR Planning," *Personnel Journal,* July 1994, 59.

78. Audrey Freedman, "Paradox: Self-interest Versus Employee Commitment," *Human Resource Forecast 1996,* (Virginia: SHRM, 1995): 13.

79. Joan Szabo, "Contract Workers: A Risky Business," *Nation's Business,* Aug. 1993, 20-24.

80. Joan Stern, telephone interview by author, Mar. 1997.

81. Stern, Mar. 1997.

82. Miller, Canfield, Paddock and Stone, P.L.C., *A Michigan Employer's Guide to Flexible Staffing* (Lansing: Michigan Chamber of Commerce, 1994), 1.

83. Miller et al., 2.

84. Society for Human Resource Management, "The Economic Environment, Growing Use of Contingent Workers," *Workplace Visions,* July/Aug. 1996, 3-4.

85. Miller et al., 2.

86. Miller et al., 2.

87. Miller et al., 13.

88. Miller et al., 14.

89. Miller et al., 15.

90. Miller et al., 21.

91. Miller et al., 21.

92. Miller et al., 23 - 24.

93. Miller et al., 24.

94. Miller et al., 59.

95. Miller et al., 62.

96. Miller et al., 62-63.

97. Miller et al., 58.

98. Miller et al., 59.

99. Miller et al, 42.

100. Miller et al., 42-43.

101. Miller et al., 43-44.

102. Miller et al., 64.

103. Miller et al., 16.

104. Miller et al., 23.

105. Miller et al., 24.

106. Judis, 6.

107. Thomas Sheeran, "Feeling Insecure," *Ann Arbor News*, 5 May 1996, E5.

108. Sheeran, E5.

109. McNerney, Donald, "Contingent Workers, Companies Refine Strategies," *HR Focus*, June 1996, 3.

110. Alan Adler, "Job Security Key to UAW's Fate," *Detroit Free Press*, 2 Sept. 1996, pp. 1A-2A.

111. *Wall Street Journal*, n.d.,1996.

112. *Wall Street Journal*.

113. James Worsham, "Labor's New Assault," *Nation's Business*, June 1997, 16-23.

114. Worsham, 16-23.

115. "Results of Outsourcing Poll," *The Advisor*, SHRM, Volume 1, Issue 2, p. 6.

116. *The Advisor*, p. 6.

117. Ronald Brownstein, "Rising Number of Self-employees Bring Changes," *Ann Arbor News*, 5 May 1996, A8.

118. *Journal of Business Strategy* quoted in John Judis, "TRB from Washington - Oracle at Delphi," *The New Republic*, 15 Apr. 1996, 6.

119. Verity, 96.

120. Valerie Frazee, "Striking a Balance: Temps and Union Workers," *Personnel Journal*, Jan. 1996, 103-105.

121. Frazee, 32.

122. Alice Lusk, "New Business from Old Clients," *Working Woman*, May 1993, 26-27.

123. Nussbaum, 130.

124. Freedman, 13.

125. Seth Kerker, "Aligning Flexible Staffing," International Quality & Productivity Center Conference Brochure, 2.

126. Brotherton, 50-55.

127. *Personnel Journal*, September 1993.

128. McKie and Lipsett, 01-44.

Glossary

This section presents a definition of the key terms as utilized in this study.

Agency Temporaries: Hired through an agency, these workers are contracted on a case-by-case, hour-per-hour basis, throughout the year to function in the same or similar capacity as regular, full-time employees. While temporary workers perform work for the outsourcing user and are exposed to their working conditions, schedules, and oftentimes work rules, they receive all remuneration (i.e., wages, benefits, withholdings, workers' compensation and unemployment compensation) from their employer (the agency).

Centralization: All decisions are made at one level or location of the organization.

Contingent Workers: Neither worker nor outsourcing user anticipate full-time regular employment. Work hours, scheduling, equipment training, supervision, and working conditions are not within the span of control of the employer.

Contracting User: The organization responsible for the selection and contracting of the worker(s).

Contract Workers: These workers are contracted by the outsourcing user to provide products/services often outside of the user's core competencies. Contracted workers have traditionally included attorneys, certified public accountants, search firms, physicians, security, janitors, and grounds maintenance workers.

Contracted Technical Workers: Contracted technical workers are highly skilled workers such as engineers, designers, scientists, or management information systems analysts. These workers often engage in long-term contracts and may be involved in global travel.

Co-op Students: These workers are students that alternate between work and school in an effort to obtain both theoretical and practical applications of knowledge and/or skills to their field of study.

Decentralization: The ability to make major and minor decisions (within defined parameters) at all levels of the organization.

Directly Hired: Directly hired workers are obtained through pre-arranged agencies, colleges, organizations, and union halls. A direct hire list could include past employees who have exhausted recall rights following work force reductions, retirees, disabled workers, apprentices, co-ops, etc.

Employee Leasing: Employee leasing occurs whenever the employer contracts with another party to employ its workers under a contract lease arrangement. The employer offering the lease arrangement is responsible for all employment-related variables as they relate to pay, benefits, and employment-related law.

Home-based Workers: These workers elect or are provided with the opportunity to work from their homes for one employer. Traditionally, these workers have been employed in telemarketing, word processing, computer programming, writing, stuffing envelopes, and/or other simple assembly.

Independent Contractors: Independent contractors are workers that work independently of the contracting user. As independents, they must successfully pass the provisions of the Internal Revenue Service 20-Factor Test, providing their own equipment, office, training, benefits, supervision, marketing, advertising, and booked hours. Independent contractors must conduct similar work for more than one employer.

Interns: Interns are students who have completed sufficient schooling to be of use to an employer by participating in specific, curriculum-related assignments involving surveys, administration, reporting, data analysis, etc.

Outsourcing: Anytime an organization goes outside the company for a service that is generally or was performed in-house, outsourcing occurs.

Outsourcing Company: This is an independent vendor company that specializes in a function of the business community such as marketing, public relations, financing, human resources, packaging, distribution, food service, security, landscaping, or janitorial services.

Part-time Work: Part-time work is employment that is less than 35 hours per week

Retirees: Retirees are mature and often well qualified workers that have completed vesting periods or career assignments and opt to return to the work force for challenging or financial reasons.

Seasonal Work: Anytime an organization experiences peaks and valleys in work patterns, this can be categorized as seasonal work. Traditionally, seasonal work is the definition applied when the work is in connection with holiday commerce, summer vacations, and fall harvesting.

In agriculture, seasonal work includes summer/fall harvesting, canning, freezing, and the shipping that follows. The demand for retail cashiers, salespeople, and stock persons spikes during the holiday season. Seasonal work also includes summer jobs for students and temporary replacements for vacation coverage.[128]

Temporary Employees: Temporary employees are workers hired with the understanding that the hours and days of their employment are of a temporary nature and may last days, weeks, or years depending upon the needs of the business. Temporary employees can be independent contractors, agency temporaries, retirees, summer co-ops, leased, and/or direct hire workers.

Temporary Work: Work of a temporary nature can include worker replacement issues such as medical, vacation, and holiday coverage; worker additions for increased production demand, special projects, or assignments; and work of a specialized nature that may not otherwise be available within the existing work force or does not demand the hours expected of a full-time worker.

Bibliography

Adler, Alan. "Job Security Vital for UAW." *Detroit Free Press*, 2 Sept. 1996, 1A-2A.

Belasco, James. *Teaching the Elephant to Dance. The Manager's Guide to Empowering Change*. New York: Plume, 1990, ISBN 0-452-26629-7.

Boyett, Joseph and Henry Conn. *Workplace 2000. The Revolution Re-shaping American Business*. New York: Plume, 1991, ISBN 0-452-26.

Brenner, Lynn. "Re-engineering Human Resources. The Disappearing HR Department." *CFO*, Mar. 1996, 61-64.

Brotherton, Phaedra. "Staff to Suit." *HR Magazine*, Dec. 1995, 50-55.

Brownstein, Ronald. "Rising Number of Self-employees Bring Changes." *Ann Arbor News*, 5 May 1996, A8.

Byrne, John. "Has Outsourcing Gone Too Far?" *Business Week*, 1 Apr. 1996, 26-28.

Caudron, Shari. "Contingent Work Force Spurs HR Planning." *Personnel Journal*, July 1994, 52-60.

Cooper, John. "Human Resources - Your Ticket to Success." *Michigan Forward*, Michigan Chamber of Commerce, July 1996, 26-27.

Druker, Peter. *Managing for the Future, the 1990's and Beyond*. New York: Dutton, Truman Talley Books 1992, ISBN 0-525-93414-6.

Flynn, Gillian. "Contingent Staffing Requires Serious Strategy." *Personnel Journal*, Apr. 1995, 50-58.

Frazee, Valerie. "Striking a Balance: Temps and Union Workers." *Personnel Journal*, Jan. 1996, 103-105.

Freedman, Audrey. "Paradox: Self-Interest Versus Employee Commitment." *Human Resources Forecast 1996*, Virginia: SHRM, 1995, 13.

Fried, Louis. *Managing Information Technology in Turbulent Times.* New York: Wiley-GED, 1995, ISBN 0-471-04742-2.

Hannon, Kerry. "The Tempting Life of a Professional Temp." 1997 Career Guide, *U.S. News & World Report*, 28 Oct. 1996, 80-81.

Harkins, Philip, Stephen Brown, and Russell Sullivan. "Shining New Light On a Growing Trend." *HR Magazine*, Dec. 1995, 75-79.

Judis, John. "TRB from Washington - Oracle at Delphi." *The New Republic*, 15 Apr. 1996, 6.

Kerker, Seth. "Aligning Flexible Staffing." International Quality & Productivity Center Conference, n.d., Brochure.

Kotter, John. *The New Rules - How to Succeed in Today's Post-corporate World.* New York: Free Press Publishing, 1995.

Kriegel, Robert and Louis Patler. *If It Ain't Broke...Break It! and Other Unconventional Wisdom for a Changing Business World.* New York: Warner Books, 1991, ISBN 0-446-39359-2.

Laabs, Jennifer. "Why HR is Turning to Outsourcing." *Personnel Journal*, Sept. 1993, 92-103.

Laabs, Jennifer. "Successful Outsourcing Depends on Critical Factors." *Personnel Journal*, Oct. 1993, 51-60.

Lusk, Alice. "New Business from Old Clients." *Working Woman*, May 1993, 26-27.

McKie, Gilmore and Laurence Lipsett. *The Contingent Worker. A Human Resources Perspective.* Virginia: SHRM, 1995, ISBN 0-939900-68-8.

McNerney, Donald. "Contingent Workers, Companies Refine Strategies." *HR Focus*, Oct. 1996, 1-6.

Naisbitt, John and Patricia Aburdene. *Megatrends 1000. Ten New Directions for the 1990's.* New York: Morrow, 1990, ISBN 0-688-07224-0.

National Association of Temporary and Staffing Services. "Tips for Controlling Costs of Contingent Staff" quoted in Phaedra Brotherton, "Staff to Suit." *HR Magazine*, Dec. 1995, 50-55.

Nelson-Nesvig, Carleen. "Getting the Most From the Leased." *The Sting*, Apr. 1995, unpublished client newsletter, 3.

Nelson-Nesvig, Carleen. "The Unions Are Coming, the Unions Are Coming." Speech presented to Phoenix Concept Alliance, Mar. 1996.

Nelson-Nesvig, Carleen. *The How to's of Human Resources*. Bee Tree Consulting Ltd., Feb. 1997.

Nollen, Stanley and Helen Axel. *Managing Contingent Workers. How to Reap the Benefits and Reduce the Risks* (New York: AMACOM, 1995) quoted in Phaedra Brotherton, "Staff to Suit." *HR Magazine*, Dec. 1995, 50-55.

Nussbaum, Bruce. "Is In-House Design On the Way Out?" *Business Week*, 25 Sept. 1995, 130.

Oliver, Suzanne. "Cut Costs, Add a Middleman." *Forbes*, 25 Apr. 1994, 135.

Olmsted, Barney and Suzanne Smith. *Creating a Flexible Workplace*. New York: AMACOM, 1989.

Phillion, Lee and John Brugger. "Encore: Retirees Give Top Performance As Temporaries." *HR Magazine*, Oct. 1994, 74-77.

"Results of Outsourcing Poll." *The Advisor*, SHRM, vol. 1, no. 2. (June 1996): 6.

Saltzman, Amy. "You, Inc." *U.S. News & World Report*, 1997 Annual Career Guide, 28 Oct. 1996, 66-79.

Sheeran, Thomas. "Feeling Insecure." *Ann Arbor News*, 5 May 1996, E5.

Spee, James. "Addition by Subtraction. Outsourcing Strengthens Business Focus." *HR Magazine*, Mar. 1995, 38-43.

Stewart, Thomas, "Taking On the Last Bureaucracy." *Fortune*, 15 Jan. 1996, 105-107.

Sunoo, Barbara Paik. "Temporary Services Create Employment Opportunities." *Personnel Journal*, July 1994, 56.

"Supplement on temporary/leased employees." Business & Legal Reports Inc., Feb. 1993.

Szabo, Joan. "Contract Workers: A Risky Business." *Nation's Business*, Aug. 1993, 20-24.

"The Growing Use of Contingent Workers." *Workplace Visions*, Society for Human Resource Management (July/Aug. 1996): 3-4.

Time Magazine, 29 Mar. 1993.

Verity, John. "They Make a Killing Minding Other People's Business." *Business Week*, 30 Nov. 1992, 96.

Verity, John. "Let's Order Out for Technology." *Business Week*, 13 May 1996, 47.

Index

Order Information

Give your potential customers, favorite chief executive officer, human resource professional, or independent contractor *Outsourcing Solutions* as a gift. To place orders, contact:

Bee Tree Consulting Ltd.
433 Bee Tree Lane
Dexter, MI 48130
(800) 427-8439 Telephone
(313) 426-7919 Fax

Please provide the following information:

NAME: _____

COMPANY NAME: _____

ADDRESS: _____

CITY/STATE/ZIP: _____

TELEPHONE: _____

Price: $12.95 each (discounts for 10 or more).

Quantity: _____

Payment Method (please check one):
   ❑ Check Enclosed   ❑ American Express
   ❑ VISA   ❑ MasterCard   ❑ Discover

Additional Products and Services:

❑ Yes, I would like to subscribe to *Moving Out*, Bee Tree Consulting Ltd.'s Quarterly Newsletter (see page 155).

❑ Please contact me regarding Bee Tree Consulting Ltd.'s human resource services.

Moving Out

A NEWSLETTER BY BEE TREE CONSULTING LTD.

Readers are encouraged to share their insights, stories, and advice for Bee Tree Consulting's new quarterly newsletter, *Moving Out*. We are specifically interested in receiving material that relates to the information already provided in *Outsourcing Solutions* or offers our readers new standards of measurement, exposures to consider, approaches that improve performance, upcoming legislative or legal issues, demographic changes, statistical information to support/reject savings, as well as success stories on integrating outsourcers into your organization.

Readers that would like to be considered for either feature articles in *Moving Out* or who wish to offer materials for future outsourcing publications are also encouraged to write. Please be specific about what information we can reprint and whether we have the right to use either your name(s) or your company name(s). Send your material to:

Bee Tree Consulting Ltd.
433 Bee Tree Lane
Dexter, MI 48130